To My Good Friend Haisha

Taking Charge begins
with Being yourself.

All my Best -

Holly L
1/13/2010

Lateral Approach **to** Taking Charge

Simple principles for new bosses on building authority and partnerships

Ho Wing Sit
And
Ling Bundgaard

Published by Lateral Approach Publishing
www.LateralApproach.com

Library of Congress Control #
2009904521 (TP); 2009904526 (HC)

Publisher's Cataloging-In-Publication Data
(Prepared by The Donohue Group, Inc.)

Sit, Ho Wing.
    Lateral approach to taking charge : simple principles for new bosses on building authority and partnerships / Ho Wing Sit and Ling Bundgaard.

        p. ; cm. -- (Lateral approach)

        ISBN: 978-0-9824689-2-0 (TP)
        ISBN: 978-0-9824689-7-5 (HC)

1. Supervisors. 2. Promotions. 3. Success in business.
I. Bundgaard, Ling. II. Title.

HF5549.12 .S58 2009
658.302   2009904526

Version 10-15-2009

2

You can only be yourself.
You will be more nervous
trying to be someone else
or
someone whom you are not.

- Ho Wing Sit

I dedicate this book to my loving wife, Ingrid, and my children Christopher and Nicholas. For my children, I believe you have the courage, the wisdom and the heart to always think of giving and contributing.

Ho Wing Sit

ACKNOWLEDGEMENTS

Nothing quite moved me to work on this book series as did my sons, Christopher and Nicholas. My wife, Ingrid, gave me the strength, luxury, and perseverance to pursue my belief. I couldn't have come this far without my co-author, Ling Bundgaard, who has long shared her breadth and depth of knowledge from working with the biggest companies around the world. I gratefully acknowledge former Lt. Governor of California, Leo T. McCarthy, former Governor of Hawaii, George R. Ariyoshi, and the many executives, mentors and "mystics" I have encountered over the years. They inspired me to embrace their values and share their wisdom. They are the ones who contributed the gems in the Lateral Approach series. My sincere thanks to Deborah Papp, my editor, who helped fine-tuned the messages while enabling me creative freedom. My special acknowledgement to my designer, Sukanya Sarkar, who helped bring the books to life through color and graphic expression.

Introduction

Lateral Approach to Taking Charge is about the powerful combination of leadership and management principles necessary to produce collaborative successes. This book is written for you if you are stepping up to a new role as manager or executive. Sometimes a promotion can be nerve racking. *"Taking Charge"* provides the basic principles and actions that can help ease the transition. Practicing these principles and actions can help you build confidence and respect from your peers, superiors, and subordinates. In a short story format, we present to you a great deal of what we have learned from our corporate Mystics and what we have experienced ourselves. We recognize the importance of these distilled experiences. We also recognize that the people who work with you, whether as managers or as peers, may one day look to you as one of their sources of wisdom.

Read this story with the intention of immediately sharing your discovery with your peers and managers. With the mind-set of sharing, practice the principles in your daily life. They apply equally to corporate and non-corporate environments.

You are reading this book because you want to know more. We hope that we enrich you with new perspectives or reinforce something you might already know.

Table of Contents

Chapter 1–The Promotion

Day 1: 3:30 PM

Alex had worked hard in a growing organization for several years, learning as much as he could on the job and aspiring to take on increased responsibilities. His good work had apparently caught the attention of John, his boss, who called Alex into his office.

As soon as Alex entered John's office, John walked up to him and gave him a welcoming pat on the back.

John said, "Alex, I have been watching you. I like what I see. I believe you are doing an excellent job and you have a lot of potential. I called you in to express my appreciation and to discuss an exciting new challenge. I am considering having you manage the Tower Project. It is not a simple project. I am thinking of setting up a new operation, which would be headed up by you. Some staff would have to be transferred and you would need to hire some new people. Of course, we will give you

11

a raise that is commensurate with your responsibility. Would you like to consider it?"

Alex tried his best to keep his cool. It was not as if he had not expected to be rewarded or recognized. Still, the good news caught him by surprise. The idea of a promotion made him feel good, very excited, and very motivated.

"Thank you, John. I have been trying to do a good job. Can you tell me a little more about this new operation you are thinking of?" Alex tried hard to contain his excitement.

"As you can imagine, the Tower Project could be quite large," John explained. "In fact, it may become the largest project our company has ever handled. However, the first phase of the project will be smaller in scope than what we normally handle. But the way we structure the project in the beginning will require us to manage and do things differently down the line. Otherwise, we will lose money instead of making a profit. In short, we will have to do more with less at first, which is the challenge I want you to take charge of," John explained.

"It is an honor to be considered. May I ask why you didn't pick Steve, Richard, or Pam, who have been with the company much longer and have proven themselves many times?" Alex inquired.

"That is a fair question. We are talking about breaking some new ground with this project, and I believe you can do a better job at that than someone who has been around for a while," John answered matter-of-factly.

Alex asked, "John, for the Tower Project to succeed, it will require Richard's and Pam's collaboration, correct?"

John acknowledged Alex's concern. "Oh yes. I will do what I can to empower you, but building successful partnerships is part of the challenge for you also, isn't it?"

"You mentioned doing more with less. Can you elaborate a little more?" Alex asked, hoping to fully understand John's expectations.

"What with globalization and outsourcing, our business environment is changing. We cannot simply follow what other people are doing. On the other hand, we must stay competitive. What I am thinking of is that we cannot simply do more of what we used to do best. Rather, we need to do things smarter to allow us to accomplish better results at less cost," John explained.

"Do you have a particular approach in mind?" Alex probed.

"I have some ideas. We can talk more as we proceed. But I want you to understand, Alex, that this is going to be your challenge." John did not want to go into too much detail before Alex had a chance to think about the offer.

None-the-less, Alex continued to dig deeper. He asked, "What about budget and resources?"

"Why don't you start putting some ideas together and we can talk more after you have given it some thought. I want to see what you can come up with that will position the company for the breakthrough we need, and how we can do more with less. I know you can do it and I am counting on you," John responded, putting the focus back on Alex's new responsibilities.

"Yes, let me give it some thought and get back to you," Alex agreed.

John seemed happy with Alex's reply. He gave Alex a firm handshake and another pat on the back as he showed him out of the room.

That night, Alex had difficulty falling asleep. Many thoughts went through his mind. First was the excitement that his hard work was being recognized. The opportunity to prove himself and be well compensated for it had arrived. He felt satisfied that his hard work had paid off. After all, that was the reason he had gone the extra mile so many times at work.

At the same time, Alex's thoughts drifted toward what was ahead for him. He began asking himself questions.

Why was I picked over the others?

Are there reasons that I don't know about?

Will the people I need to work with cooperate with me?

Will the people I manage follow me?

What do I really know about the project?

What are my chances for success?

What did John really mean by doing more with less?

What breakthroughs does John have in mind?

Can I do it?

Such questions kept Alex awake most of the night. He couldn't quite sort them all out. He really felt the need to talk to someone. While he had a lot of respect and trust for John, doubts still lingered.

Suddenly, Alex remembered that John always talked about a "Mystic" who is very knowledgeable about management matters. He decided his next step would be to pay this

Mystic a visit. With that thought, Alex finally fell asleep.

The Promotion

Chapter 2 – Be Yourself

Day 2: 11:00 AM

Alex was a little nervous when he approached the Mystic's office at the appointed time. The receptionist offered Alex coffee, but he declined. He paced back and forth pretending to look at the mementos hanging on a wall. In fact, Alex was wondering if he had made a mistake coming here. He wondered how to present his case and whether the Mystic could help. After all, what could he say about the Tower Project? What could he know about what John was thinking? What could he know about what Alex needed to do?

The Mystic stepped out from his office with his hand extended and a smile on his face.

"You must be Alex. It is nice to meet you."

"Thank you for finding the time to meet with me on such short notice," Alex responded. "I hope I won't waste your time."

Alex shook the Mystic's hand hesitantly. As if the Mystic understood Alex's ambivalent feelings, he quickly alleviated the awkward situation.

"Well, my congratulations to you on your promotion. I don't know if I can help, but I will be happy to share some of my experience if it's needed. We won't know unless we get started, will we?"

"I am not sure I know where to begin," Alex answered.

"Why don't you start by telling me a little about yourself?" the Mystic prompted.

Alex began by telling the Mystic about his professional background and what work he did at his company.

"I started working for the company about three years ago. Overall, the company has treated me well. I have worked hard and I believe I've done a good job. There have been times when I have felt that the company could recognize my contributions a little more and pay me a little more generously, but now, with this promotion, I don't know what to think. The company is asking me to manage an important project and form a new organization. I am excited, but I have other mixed feelings. To begin with, my academic training wasn't in management. I really have no formal management training to speak of. What I know, I learned from reading books and from on-the-job experience. I always believed that I could do more and I wanted challenges. But I am not sure if I can do a good job at what the company is asking me to do right now. Although I was hoping for a promotion, this promotion and the challenge that comes along with it caught me by surprise. I have questions I can't answer."

"So you feel this is the opportunity you were working toward but you question whether or not you can do it," the Mystic empathized. "Go on and tell me more."

"Well, our company has many more experienced, more senior people than me around. I am not sure why John, my boss, picked me for this project," Alex began.

"So you feel there are more experienced managers around, and you wonder if there are other reasons you have been picked. Go on and tell me more," the Mystic continued, prompting Alex to open up.

"The project I am to lead is called the Tower Project. I have been somewhat involved up to this point, but not to a great extent. It is expected to be a very difficult project. I am expected to set up a new organization just for this project. I am not sure of my chance for success." Alex started to pick up speed as he spoke, sensing that the Mystic was catching on to how he was feeling.

"So you feel your assignment will be very difficult, there are many unknowns, and you don't know if you can succeed. Please go on," the Mystic encouraged.

"John also said that we must do more with less and he wants me to break new ground. I am not sure what he expects."

"So you feel that John's expectations are also an unknown," the Mystic acknowledged. "Please go on."

"These are some of the questions that are bothering me and I wonder if you have any insights you can share with me." Alex was relieved that he had asked the most troublesome questions, and he paused.

The Mystic slowly leaned forward. He looked Alex straight in the eye and with somewhat of a gentle smile said to him, "Well, I will be happy to answer your questions and share my insights in good time. But these are not the kinds of questions you should be asking at this time. At this moment in time, all you need to know is that you are being called upon to lead, so you must be yourself."

"What do you mean, be myself?" Alex was surprised by the Mystic's response.

"At this moment in time, Jack Welch, Andy Grove, Edward Deming, Rockefeller, Carnegie, or any other leader in the business world may

23

not be able to perform your assignment as effectively as you can," the Mystic replied.

Alex looked at the Mystic bewildered. He liked what he heard, but he was not certain he had heard it right.

"How is that possible?" he asked. "I read their books. They have all achieved so much. In fact, some of them are my idols."

"Oh yes, many of them are my idols also, and I study their work as well. Under certain circumstances, everyone can become a leader. This is your moment. For the task at hand, I am not sure if anyone else can necessarily do a better job than you can," the Mystic answered, reminding Alex of a basic principle of leadership.

"Really! Is that why you told me to be myself?" Alex felt more assured and responded accordingly.

"Yes, because you are not them. Even if you were at their level or in their position, you would not want to be them, either. What you really want is to learn from them and leverage their experience. Above all, what you want is to be yourself. Besides, your choice is very limited, isn't it?" the Mystic continued to explain.

Alex began to understand. "I didn't think of it that way, but I believe you are absolutely right. I can only be myself. I would be more nervous trying to be someone I am not."

"Alex, you have the right idea. But I do want you to remember something," the Mystic continued.

"What is that?" Alex asked.

"Never believe that you are entitled to lead," the Mystic cautioned.

"Oh! Why is that?" Alex answered, surprised.

"You only have an opportunity. While you are at the helm, you should treat every day as if it is your first day on the job. Leadership can be very transient. The current need for your leadership may subside until new needs arise that call on you to lead again. If you adopt this philosophy, you can adapt to changes in circumstances with greater peace of mind," the Mystic emphasized.

Alex did not catch on. "Are you saying that a leader's job is not secure?"

"No. What I am saying is that you need not lead every single day and on every matter in order to be respected as a leader. You are called upon to lead right now. So, you need not hesitate. Go ahead and provide leadership. The day will come when it will be someone else's turn. When that day arrives, move on. There will always be an abundance of opportunities for good leaders," the Mystic explained.

"I am glad you are pointing this out to me. Now I feel a level of comfort at accepting the promotion. I will use this opportunity to refine my leadership skills." Alex felt encouraged and his perspective on the promotion started to change.

"Alex, how do you plan to manage?" the Mystic inquired, leading the way for continued guidance.

"Manage? I thought I've been asked to take on a leadership role," Alex answered.

"In today's business environment, it is rare to have a position that purely calls for leadership alone. Usually, it is a combination of leadership and management. The two roles are, in fact, different. The skills associated with them are different. Knowing when leadership is called for and when management takes over may cause some confusion to most people. So how do you plan to manage?" the Mystic repeated.

"I haven't thought about that yet." Alex still did not give the Mystic the answer he was looking for.

Finally, the Mystic pointed to a book on top of his desk and asked, "By the way, has John been practicing the Lateral Approach to creating success?"

"Do you mean managing by values? Yes." Alex felt a little embarrassed and he smiled as he answered.

"Can you tell me how John manages?" The Mystic smiled as well. He knew Alex understood where he was taking the conversation. None-the-less, the Mystic continued to check on the depth of Alex's understanding.

"John's core philosophy is to create success for everyone. That made me respects him. He manages by only three values. They are very easy to understand and follow and John made it clear to everyone that these are his rules. Value #1 says we are to make and meet commitments and set challenging goals. Value #2 directs us to properly plan, budget, and staff projects. Value #3 asks us to pay attention to details and take pride in our work. These values help us to define, prepare, and execute for success. It is quite effective." Alex's confidence increased as he explained his understanding of the principles of managing by values.

"So, do you think managing by values will be just as effective for you in your situation?" the Mystic asked.

"I don't see why not. I understand and live by these values," Alex quickly answered.

"Good, Alex, then you knows the fundamentals for creating success for the Tower Project. That may be one of the reasons you were picked," the Mystic said, indirectly answering one of the questions Alex had asked earlier.

"Thanks for your assurance," Alex answered with sincerity.

The Mystic suddenly became very serious. "Alex, if it is your intention to accept the promotion from John, you have to think about taking charge. There are certain actions you will need to take with expedience. Think about that and come back to see me early tomorrow. You need to act now."

"That is a lot to think about. Where should I begin?" Alex asked.

"Why don't you start with your first set of meetings?" the Mystic suggested.

"Oh, that would be easy enough," Alex said confidently. The Mystic gave Alex a little smile. He extended his hand to say good-bye. Alex did the same.

As Alex walked away, he examined his feelings. He felt glad that he had come even though many of his questions had not been answered. He felt a new set of priorities had been identified. He also felt that what he had heard about the Mystic's ability to help was correct. He did not know exactly why, but he felt comfortable talking to him. As a result of the conversation, he felt more certain and more confident of himself.

The rest of the day, many thoughts continued to go through Alex's mind. He followed the Mystic's suggestion and focused his energy on how to take charge of the people he would soon be meeting with on the project and his new role. Alex began to realize that, unlike meetings in the past, the upcoming meeting would be a little bit more complex. What would he say to John and how should he establish a new relationship with him? How should he position himself with his future managers, with whom he had worked side-by-side only yesterday? What should he say and how should he say it to the rest of the staff?

Alex worked hard that day making preparations. Although he still could not answer all the questions swimming around in his brain, unlike the night before, he felt at ease that he was moving in the right direction. He had a good night's sleep.

Alex reflected on the conversation, and entered into his notebook the following:

Be Yourself

- All you need to know is that you are being called upon to lead, so be yourself.
- Under certain circumstances, everyone can become a leader. This is your moment. For the task at hand, no one else can necessarily do a better job than you can.
- What you really want is to learn and leverage the experience of your business role models. Above all, you want to be yourself. Besides, your choice is very limited.
- You can only be yourself. You will be more nervous trying to be someone else or someone whom you are not.
- Never have the false belief that you are entitled to lead. You only have an opportunity. While you are at the helm, you should treat every day as if it is your first day on the job.
- The leadership role can be very transient. The current needs for your leadership may subside until new needs arise for you to lead again. If you adopt this philosophy, you can adapt to changes in different circumstances with peace of mind.

- You need not lead every single day and on every matter in order for you to be respected as a leader.
- When you are called upon to lead, you need not hesitate. Go ahead and provide the leadership.
- The day will come where it may be someone else's turn. When that day arrives, move on. There will always be an abundance of opportunities for good leaders.
- In today's business, it is rare to have a position that purely calls for leadership alone. Usually, it is a combination of leadership and management. The two roles are, in fact, different. The skills associated with them are different. Knowing when leadership is called for and when management takes over may cause some confusion to most people.
- Knowing the fundamentals to creating success may be one of the reasons you were picked for a promotion.
- If your intention is to accept a promotion, you have to think about taking charge. There are certain actions you need to take with expedience.

Chapter 3 – Manage and Be Managed

Day 3: 8:00 AM

Alex arrived at the Mystic's office at the appointed time. After the usual pleasantries, he and the Mystic got down to business.

"I can tell that you had a good night's rest, so I suppose you've made good progress at determining how to get started with taking charge. So tell me what you've come up with," the Mystic said.

"Well, I have a lot of ideas about how to run the Tower Project. First, I plan to share my ideas with John, my future managers, and staff," Alex said excitedly.

"That's very good. It seems like you are starting to see the possibilities. Please go on," the Mystic encouraged.

"More than that, although I have not put them down on paper yet, I have developed goals and plans." Alex continued to share the work he did yesterday.

"That is even better. It seems like you not only know what to do, you also know how to do it. Please go on," the Mystic continued.
"As far as taking charge is concerned, I am a straight shooter, so I plan to come right out and tell my future managers and staff that this is our mission, this is our plan, and that I am now in charge of it," said Alex. "I think a quick and direct delivery will be effective."

"You think doing it your way will enable you to take charge more effectively. Please go on."

Again, Alex spoke with conviction. "As far as John is concerned, I will tell him that I accept his offer, and would like his commitment to continue to support my project."

"You want John to commit to executive support of your project," the Mystic confirmed. "Please go on."

"This way, with my boss backing me up, I can quickly take charge. What do you think?" Alex asked.

"That is one approach. What do you think John's reaction would be if you were to explain it to him?" the Mystic asked.

Alex felt a little defensive. "Why? John asked me to take the helm, and I am doing exactly what he asked me to do. What can be wrong with that?"

"It is not about right or wrong," the Mystic explained, introducing a new idea. "It is more about 'Manage and Be Managed'."

"What is 'Manage and Be Managed'?" Alex was a little surprised and confused.

"'Manage and Be Managed' is a balancing act you must quickly learn. If you want to immediately reinforce John's confidence in his decision to select you for this project, you must let yourself be managed by John."

"But, John has always been my manager. What has changed?" Alex asked.

"Your role has changed," explained the Mystic. "Now that John has given you a longer leash, more power, and more freedom to make decisions, the first thing you need to do is to make sure he feels that he is more in control of you."

Alex was perplexed. "Oh. But I thought he wants me to take the helm."

"Alex, everyone must answer to somebody. You know that, don't you?" the Mystic asked with a smile.

"Not John. He is the senior vice president," Alex replied emphatically.
"Oh, but he does. He has to answer to the president and CEO," the Mystic challenged.

"What about the president and CEO?" Alex challenged back. "Whom do they answer to?"

"They answer to the board of directors," the Mystic quickly replied.

"What about the board of directors?" Alex continued.

"They answer to the shareholders," the Mystic quickly replied.

"What about the shareholders?" Alex wouldn't give up.

"It might sound funny, but they answer to their spouses and children." The Mystic almost burst out laughing as he answered. Alex could not help but laugh along.

"What about the President of the United States?" Alex challenged once again.

The Mystic looked at Alex and calmly answered his challenge. "The President of the United States answers to you. You probably cast a vote for or against him, right?"

Alex finally caught on. "I think I get it. By letting myself be managed, I can build confidence and trust with my boss. By doing this, I can actually empower myself to do even more."

"Alex, you have it. **The higher the level you go, the more you have to be conscious of being controllable.**"

Alex began to see the implications and was able to answer his own questions that had been puzzling him so much. "Maybe this is another reason why John picked me over the others. He and I always get along well and I like to ask him for advice and let him know what I am doing. To John, I am manageable and he knows he can manage me."

"Very good! This may very well be one of the reasons why John picked you," the Mystic agreed.

"So how do I let myself be managed in this new situation?" Alex wanted to know more.

"As you told me in our last meeting, you are not sure what John expects of you. Isn't it time to be a good listener?" the Mystic asked.

"I plan to do that. John hasn't told me much so far," Alex answered.

"Alex, don't expect too much. If John is thinking at the level I anticipate, he will probably give you a general idea of what he expects. He gave you the promotion so that you can give him answers, sort of like filling in the blanks. Not that John does not know how to that, but he perceives it as your job now," the Mystic cautioned.

"Is that good or bad?" Alex asked.

"It is good. That is what empowerment is all about. By the way," the Mystic added casually, "how have you been managing John?"

Alex was perplexed. "Wait just a minute. What do you mean by managing John? John is my boss."

"That is just what I mean. How have you been managing your boss?" the Mystic persisted.

"But John has been managing me. I don't think I can manage my boss." Alex was not catching on.

"Well, people manage their bosses every day. Think of it this way: if you forgot your wedding anniversary, would you try to do something to make it up to your wife?"

"Well, yes," Alex acknowledged.

"You would try to manage her mood, right?" the Mystic probed.

"That is true," Alex agreed.

"When CEO's and presidents make forward-looking statements about the state of the company, are they managing their shareholders' expectations?"

"Yes," Alex agreed.

"When employees ask their bosses for a raise, aren't they managing their bosses' perception of their value?" the Mystic continued.

"That is very true. I am starting to understand what you mean." Alex was now convinced.

"As you see, I am not saying you should step over your boss or over-step him, either. You should never do that. After all, he is your boss and you should pay him the proper respect," the Mystic cautioned, to make sure Alex understood.

"Is that what you mentioned earlier about it being a balancing acting between managing and being managed?"

"Alex, you are good," the Mystic encouraged. "That is the balancing act between 'Manage and Be Managed'."

"I like it. You have opened up my eyes." Alex was pleased with his understanding of this new concept.

"Of course," the Mystic added, "as your management skills become more refined, the less your boss, John, will feel that he is being managed."

"So, what you are saying is that John should still feel in full control so that he will bless whatever comes up," Alex reiterated.

"Yes. 'Manage and Be Managed' has some pretty major implications," the Mystic continued.

"What are the implications?" Alex asked.

"If you are successful managing and being managed by your own boss, you can determine your own success and rely less on your boss or the abilities of your boss," responded the Mystic.

"I can see that. I have heard many associates of mine complaining about their bosses. They feel that they have no opportunity to advance because of their bosses' shortcomings," Alex related. "It seems like this can no longer be an excuse."

"That may very well be true. Of course, many factors can contribute to someone's inability to advance. Opportunities may be limited at the corporate level or departmental level, for example. The principle of 'Manage and Be Managed', however, turns problems into opportunities and leverages strengths into new and better opportunities," the Mystic explained.

"How can I apply what you just said to my situation?" Alex asked.

"You mentioned that you have goals and plans in mind. Why don't you work with John on developing them as a way to get started?" the Mystic suggested.

"You want to be managed by listening to what John has to say about his expectations, his goals, his plans, etc. You want to be managed by leveraging John's expectations, goals, and plans to combine with yours. This way, both of you come to total agreement on how the project will be handled." The Mystic laid out the win-win scenario.

Puzzled, Alex asked, "If John already has his own expectations, goals, and plans, why should mine be different?"

Patiently, the Mystic further explained. "Alex, you are the one who has to execute, not John. If you are not in total agreement with each other, both of you are set up to fail. So you had better tactfully speak up and make sure there are no misunderstandings right from the start."

"If I am the one to be responsible for execution, why wouldn't John follow my expectations, goals, and plans?" Alex asked.

"Chances are John would give you the benefit of the doubt. That is the likely scenario. But keep in mind, both of you must be in total agreement. After all, he is your champion. He has to believe in what you are doing. At the end of the day, he is the ultimate responsible party," the Mystic replied.

"But we don't necessarily see everything the same way," Alex continued to challenge. "How can we get to the point of total agreement?"

"The situation you describe happens often. If you are in doubt, it is absolutely OK to follow John and be managed. If you are confident enough, you should stand up, be counted, and manage," said the Mystic, adding, "Of course, it is when you chose to manage that you set yourself up to be either a hero or a goat. Once again, it is a balancing act."

Still concerned with respect to managing his boss, Alex asked, "If John was aware that he was being managed, wouldn't he feel that I was sneaky or that I couldn't be trusted?"

The Mystic's answer was a little surprising. "I would say it is just the reverse. He would respect you more. 'Manage and Be Managed' is not some backhanded technique. It is a principle for building consensus and relationships. It applies to the relationship between you and your subordinates as well as you and your boss."

"Me and my subordinates?" Not surprisingly, the Mystic's answer was somewhat confusing to Alex.

"Of course. If you are managing your boss, wouldn't you expect your subordinates to be managing you?" the Mystic answered logically.

"That is true," Alex acknowledged.

Moving a little closer to Alex, the Mystic looked at him and asked, "If your subordinates were savvy enough to openly lead you to see things their way, wouldn't you respect them for it? These are your potential future managers and executives, the movers and the shakers, aren't they?"

"I guess you are right," answered Alex, convinced.
Returning to Alex's original question, the Mystic continued. "With John's experience, do not think for a minute that he does not know what you are doing. John will respect what you are doing because you are doing it to make everyone successful, aren't you?"

"Absolutely! I have no other objective but to make everyone successful," Alex answered emphatically.

"Well, let's put this to work. Will you be meeting with John soon?" the Mystic asked.

"Yes, later today," Alex answered.

"What do you plan to do when you meet with John?" the Mystic inquired.

"As a result of my conversation today with you, I plan to do more listening and less talking," Alex confirmed.

The Mystic provided Alex with more guidance. "You mentioned that you already have plans and goals, so why don't you think about the three most critical items you need John to be in agreement with and ask him what he thinks?"

"Great idea!" Alex acknowledged.

The Mystic clapped his hands together and nodded his head to show his encouragement. "Good, I think you are ready to talk to John. Go, and let me know the results."

"Thank you so much. I think I am ready." Alex gave the Mystic a smile as he prepared to leave.

Alex reflected on his conversation with the Mystic. He entered into his notebook the following:

Manage and Be Managed

- With respect to your boss, is not about whether you are right or wrong. Often, it is more about managing and being managed.
- 'Manage and Be Managed' is a balancing act you must quickly learn. If you want to quickly gain your boss's confidence that he made the right choice by selecting you for the promotion, let yourself be managed.
- When your boss gives you a longer leash, more power, and more freedom of action, it becomes more important to make your boss feel that he is in control.
- Building confidence and trust with your boss can empower yourself to do more.
- The higher the level you go, the more you have to be conscious of being controllable.
- Everyone must answer to somebody.
- Allowing yourself to be managed and manageable may be one of the management promotion preferences.
- He gave you the promotion so that you can give him answers. Not that you boss does not know

the answers, but he will perceive it as your job now.

- Managing and being managed by your boss includes expectations, goals, plans, etc. In this respect people manage their bosses everyday, and are also managed by their bosses.

- Managing your boss does not mean stepping over your boss or overstepping him, either. You should never do that. After all, he is your boss and you must pay him the proper respect.

- 'Manage and Be Managed' is not some backhanded technique. It is a principle for building consensus and relationships. It applies to the relationship between you and your subordinates as well as you and your boss.

- Do not think for a minute that your boss does not know that you are managing his expectations, goals, plans, etc. On the contrary, your boss respects what you are doing, and you are doing your job to make everyone successful.

- If your subordinates are savvy enough to openly lead you to seeing things their way, you should give them the proper respect. These are your potential future managers and executives, the movers and shakers.

- If you are successful managing and being

managed by your own boss, you can determine your own success and rely less on your boss or the abilities of your boss.

- Many factors can limit someone's ability to advance. The limited opportunity may be at the corporate level or departmental level. Their bosses may contribute to it also. The principle of 'Manage and Be Managed' turns problems into opportunities and leverages strengths into new and additional opportunities.

- Without total agreement between you and your boss, both of you are set up to fail. So you had better tactfully speak up and make sure there are no misunderstandings.

- You and your boss don't necessary see everything the same way. If you are in doubt, it is absolutely OK to follow your boss and be managed. If you are confident, you should stand up, be counted, and manage. When you chose to manage, that's where you will either be the hero or the goat.

- If you are managing your boss, you should expect your subordinates to be doing the same thing: that is, managing their boss, which is you.

-

Chapter 4 – Meeting With Your Boss

Day 3: 1:00 PM

Alex had a quick sandwich in his cubicle while he went over his notes from his visits with the Mystic. He quickly modified his multi-page list of plans and reduced his ideas down to a few bullets and a brief explanation to fit on a single page. He went over his summary and mentally practiced his delivery of the messages. Finally, he had one goal in mind and three things he needed John's agreement on.

Alex set a goal to double return on investment by cutting the prospect-to-bill cycle time by half. To do that, he wanted John to agree with:

- Assigning David to Alex's team, where he would serve as his right hand
- Building a new tiger sales team
- Getting Engineering's cooperation

While Alex actually had a list of many other things, he felt that these three were key to a successful Tower Project.

53

On his way to John's office, Alex reminded himself to listen instead of talk. Reaching John's office, he knocked on the open door and poked his head inside. John looked up with a smile and said, "There you are, Alex. Come on in."

"Well, have you thought over what we talked about? It is a promotion you know!" John teased.

Alex responded with a sincere thank you as he accepted John's offer. "I cannot thank you enough. I appreciate your trust in me. I will be happy to accept the promotion and I hope I will do a great job. Having said that, there is still a lot you need to share with me."

"What do you want to know?" John leaned back in his chair and adjusted his position as he awaited Alex's questions.

"Let's start with your expectations of me and the project," replied Alex with careful deliberation and a little excitement.

John responded, "As I said before, the Tower Project has the potential to be quite large. As a matter of fact, it may become the largest project our company has ever handled. On the other hand, the first phase of the project is slightly below the size we normally handle. The way we structure the project will require us to manage and do some other things differently. Otherwise, we may lose money instead of make a profit. In short, we have to do more with less. Overall, this is our longer-term business direction. So what I expect of you is to make this project a success by making it profitable."

"Do you have anything in particular in mind that we should be aware of when we bid for the project that you believe will make the project profitable?" Alex followed up.

"The bid was based on Bob's concept," John explained, going into some history of the project. "Unfortunately, several of the assumptions turned out to be either not executable or not accurate. I am no longer comfortable with the concept and approach."

Hoping that John would provide more guidance and direction, Alex asked, "But what do you think? You mentioned that you have some ideas."

"Bob's outsourcing concept needs to be reviewed. I am not against the concept of outsourcing entirely, but we have to be smart about what to leverage and how to leverage. After all, we have to think globally," John answered.

Remembering the Mystic's lesson on 'Manage and Be Managed', Alex set the tone for an open dialog.
"Why don't you and I work together on this very critical issue? I need your guidance and support in this area," he suggested.

"Good idea. It is a strategic issue and we need to take a cautious approach. We need to take it one step at a time and still be very aggressive," John agreed.

"Good, let me do some homework and get back to you on my findings," Alex responded, preparing himself to be managed by John and offering to do the more tedious work that John probably shouldn't be doing at his level.

"Yes, Alex, do that." John nodded his head and gave Alex a smile, obviously happy that Alex was demonstrating responsive and responsible leadership.

Following up on John's earlier comment with respect to outsourcing, Alex led the conversation to the three items he needed John's support for.

"John, isn't the whole outsourcing question really about making some breakthroughs in Engineering and our method of production? As I was working on putting together a plan, this became an area of concern for me. That is, I feel that the success of the Tower Project is highly dependent on the cooperation of the Engineering group. Do you agree that Engineering needs to collaborate very closely with us?"

Apparently, obtaining Engineering's cooperation was on John's mind also. "I am glad you brought this up. This is one of the keys to the project's success. We have to make sure that Engineering collaborates and has clear responsibilities. Alex, you might consider including design experts on your team so that we have control on the general direction from the beginning. What do you think?"

"That is something to think about. Engineering may not like it that a new operation would have its own design expertise. If I can get their support, perhaps it will speed things up. Do you agree?" Alex was happy that John was thinking along the same lines as him, but continued to defer to John and solicit John's opinions.

"I think it will speed things up. Why don't we plan on talking to Engineering together?" As Alex had expected, John gave a definitive answer.

"John, what do you think about David?" Alex moved on to the next item on his priority list.

"What are you thinking of?" John questioned.

"I am thinking about building the Tower Project team. I am thinking of including someone who can run fast and cover areas I might not be as strong in, like technologies," Alex explained.

"What about Patrick? He is strong in technologies," John suggested.

"Patrick and I haven't been on the front line together before. He may be better in certain areas than David. But I know David, and I know he can manage and is manageable," Alex countered.

"So you value someone whom you understand and have worked with before. Yes, you might be able to run faster since you two have already warmed up. That will work. Go ahead; put him on your team. Do you have anyone else in mind for your team?" After listening to Alex's reasoning, John was comfortable giving Alex the go-ahead.

"Let me put together a list so that you can take a look. David is a key person as far as I am concerned." Alex was careful to take the opportunity to defer to John to bless the people he wanted on his team. Alex wanted to make sure John felt he was in control.

"Alex, you should think about using Ed, also," John suggested.
"I don't know Ed that well. Let me talk to him. What do you like about Ed?" As Alex answered, he remembered the Mystic's advice about it being absolutely OK to be managed when in doubt.

"Ed is quite creative. He can be useful to you," John answered.

"Let's try to integrate him into the team, then. Who else would you suggest?" Alex asked.

"Let me think about it," John replied.

Alex continued the conversation with another question. "Can you think of other important issues and actions that I should be addressing right away?"

"Actually there are quite a few items in Engineering, and in Services and Sales, also," John responded. "We touched on some items in Engineering, such as outsourcing and the management of product design. We need to also think about our installation and support methods in order to become more efficient and lower our costs. We still have to sell the subsequent phases of this project. Our success is not defined only by executing the current phase. If we were to change our corporate direction, we would need to make it scalable and marketable in order to beat our competition."

John's answer indicated that he had already given this new operation a lot of serious thought and that there was a lot he wanted to accomplish. Alex was becoming a little overwhelmed as he continued to listen intently.

"Would it be difficult to convince our current sales team to change the way they sell? Would it be more effective to train someone with sales experience to follow us throughout the project and be on hand to speak to our prospect with conviction? What do you think?" Alex led John toward the next priority on his list.

"I am not sure. That would be a little complex organizationally. The Sales organization has assigned territories and quotas. Your suggestion may be disruptive," John pointed out.

"Shouldn't we be thinking ahead? If we are to move quickly on this project, won't we have to face this issue very quickly?" Alex challenged.

"You may be right, Alex. We have to consider this now rather than later. Let me talk to Sales." John felt that Alex's suggestion was worth exploring.

Alex continued to share some of his out-of-the box ideas. "Our objective is to help the company do more business and to make the Sales organization a success. Anything we do to organize or reorganize is for the purpose of maximizing returns for the company. If we can structure incentives so that Sales is receptive, would that work?"

John seemed to be enjoying the brainstorming. "It is possible," he replied. "Perhaps your team can train the sales force or create consultants or something like that. There is some work to be done here."

Alex was pleased with John's response. Out of the three items on his list, they were already in full agreement on two of them. Alex believed that eventually, there would also be a good solution on the last remaining item.

At this point, Alex took out his single page summary with the three critical items he believed must be accomplished in order for the project to succeed. He went through the summary in checklist fashion, looked up, and handed his summary to John. He waited while John quickly glanced at it.

"By the way, what kind of results are you expecting, John?" Alex asked.

"We need to do things smarter. We need to accomplish better results for less cost. What do you think you can achieve?" John wasn't as specific as Alex had hoped he would be.
Careful not to over commit, Alex shared his estimates. "Well I gave it some thought. It is very preliminary, but we may be able to double

the return on investment by cutting the prospect-to-bill cycle time by half. Now don't hold me to this yet. But this is the magnitude that I will be creating a plan against. It is going to be a challenging goal. And once our team makes a commitment to it, I plan to meet that commitment."

As Alex had hoped, John was obviously delighted by what he was hearing.

"Alex, if we can achieve something of this magnitude, then we certainly will have a breakthrough."

Alex quickly summarized. "There is quite a bit to think about. I have a preliminary plan in mind. Let me organize the plan and run it by you first. I feel my priority is to build my core team. I feel that I need to meet with the key people who will be on our team and instill in them the importance of owning the project plan. Am I approaching it the way you would?" he asked.

"That's what I like about you, Alex," John answered. "I feel that you understand me and we can work well together."

John had been observing Alex carefully and felt satisfied that Alex knew what he was talking about. He also felt Alex had done his homework. He was comfortable with his decision to promote Alex and his confidence in his decision took another step forward.

Chapter 5 – Roles and Responsibilities of a Manager

Day 3: 5:00 PM

As Alex walked into the Mystic's office, it was obvious that the Mystic was as excited to see Alex as Alex was to see the Mystic.

The Mystic quickly shook hands with Alex and asked, "Well, how did it go with John?"

"Better than expected," Alex relied proudly. "I followed your instructions to do more listening and less talking. I did ask my share of leading questions. I also took extra steps to let myself be managed."

"Good, go on," the Mystic prompted.

"Today, John seems somewhat different than usual. He seems to be more hands-on than before," Alex continued, sharing the small surprise he had experienced.

"Why are you surprised? Did you report directly to John before?" the Mystic asked.

67

"Yes," Alex answered. "But today, he seems to be more open and we had a good discussion." "Now that he promoted you and is assigning you an important project, wouldn't you agree that John cannot afford *not* to work with you in overseeing this project?" the Mystic prompted.

Alex seemed to understand. "I see," he said.

"What else did you do in your meeting with John?" the Mystic continued.

"I followed your suggestion. Before I went to the meeting, I made sure I had narrowed down the items John and I must have complete agreement on." Alex wanted to make sure that the Mystic understood that he had followed his suggestion.

"Did you get John to agree?" the Mystic questioned.

"Yes, on two out of three items," Alex explained. "On building a tiger sales team under me, which John indicated he needs to do a little more thinking about. John will be talking to Sales. I believe if I were to be responsible for hitting our goal of reducing the prospect-to-bill cycle by half, John would support me in whatever I needed."

The Mystic seemed satisfied. "It sounds like you will work together on a solution. Good. What else?"

"While I was listening and making sure that I was opening myself up to be managed, I think I managed John's expectations and influenced his thinking. We established a good and very comfortable exchange," Alex emphasized. "I think John respects me for what I was doing; especially after I handed him my summary."

"So John knew that you were prepared and that there were specific items you wanted him to agree to," the Mystic confirmed.

"Yes, I was very open and forthright about what I had been able to accomplish so far." Alex felt good as he explained his approach.

"Very good, you are progressing very fast. You've learned that it isn't out of the question to be able to manage your boss and gain respect at the same time, haven't you?" the Mystic encouraged.

"The preparation sure makes a difference. I feel happy that John and I actually enjoyed working together." Alex associated his success with John to his preparation for the meeting with him.

"Now that you have the support from your boss, what do you think your next step will be?" the Mystic asked Alex, moving on to the next subject.

"I plan to begin by talking to David. I plan to talk to him about this project. It is time to build my team," Alex explained.

"Good. How would you start?" the Mystic asked.

"John agreed with me to bring David on. I plan to make him my right hand person. John suggested I use Ed, also. I agreed to talk to Ed. As you suggested for a situation in which I wasn't sure, I just followed my boss. It seemed a natural thing to do," Alex recounted.

"Sounds like you know David well already. What will he be doing for you?" the Mystic asked.

"He will help me to manage a part of the team," Alex continued.

"So he will be managing. Has he managed people before?" the Mystic continued.

"Yes and no. He and I fought many battles in the trenches in the past. I know him well and he gets things done. In that respect, he has managed people," Alex responded a little hesitantly.

"Can I assume that you can recruit David to your team? That you can excite and inspire him to join this project?" the Mystic continued to challenge.
"Yes, I think I can," Alex answered.

"Same for Ed after you talk to him?" the Mystic continued.

"Yes," Alex answered.

"After you recruit them to your team, will you be clarifying their roles and responsibilities?" the Mystic asked, introducing a new idea.

Alex was a little puzzled. "What do you mean? As I said, I will make them managers, and that will be their role. After we create the plan, then their assignments will also be very clear."

"That is a common assumption. Wouldn't there be more?" the Mystic probed.

"I don't understand." Alex was feeling very puzzled now.

"Alex, as I said, your role has changed. First you must elevate your level of management and start taking charge. If David and Ed are to be a part of your management team, they have much more responsibility than what you just mentioned, correct? Failure to be clear on their roles and responsibilities will rest on you," the Mystic explained.

"Oh, what are these responsibilities?" Alex asked.

"Let's start with the subject of communication. It is more involved than most people realize. Wouldn't you want to be clear on what and how David and Ed are to communicate with you? Wouldn't you want to lay down the rules of engagement right from the start?" The Mystic began to guide Alex.

"That's right," Alex agreed.

"Wouldn't you want to make sure that they understand how you plan to manage also?" the Mystic continued.

Alex agreed again.

"Wouldn't you want to let them know your expectations for the project and their performance?" the Mystic guided.

"That's also important." Alex was beginning to see the complexity.

"The same applies to subordinates. What about David's and Ed's method of communication and management of their subordinates?" The Mystic continued to identify the many perspectives of communication.

He went on. "What about communication with the clients?"

"Very important." Once again, Alex nodded his head and agreed quietly.

"I think you get the point that managing communication is more involved. I don't imagine that David or Ed is trained on many aspects of communication. Educating them will be your responsibility. You should start right away. This process empowers you to take charge sooner," the Mystic explained.

"So that is part of the Lateral Approach to taking charge?" Alex questioned.

"Yes, because you will gain respect by bringing to your team's attention their challenges as well as instructing them on something they should know but don't. If your team understands what you are doing, it is almost like putting money in their pocket," said the Mystic.

What the Mystic was saying captured Alex's attention, and now he wanted to know more.

"I didn't realize the significance," he said. "What could be other important items to educate my team on?"

"Do you know that you can't expect to achieve a breakthrough or make important changes without reshaping people's thinking, attitude, approach, and habits?" the Mystic responded, calling out another important point.

"Yes, I am counting on the people I selected to have the right thinking, attitude, approach, and habits needed to achieve a breakthrough," Alex acknowledged.

"Well, you will probably find that some of the people may meet your needs. That wouldn't be enough to change an organization or business direction. In order to get everyone on board, you need to educate all your managers so that they can, in turn, properly educate their subordinates. Wouldn't that be so?" the Mystic continued.

"When you put it that way, I can see the work and challenge that is ahead of me," Alex commented.

The Mystic continued. "Wouldn't your clients need educating also? Wouldn't they, too, have to understand your new approach or methodology?"

"Educating our clients will be half the battle," Alex agreed.

"Wouldn't people in other departments need educating also? They won't be able to support you as effectively if they don't understand what you really need and where you are heading, will they?" the Mystic added.

"They would be more effective if the people we interact with understand what we need and know where we are heading," Alex acknowledged.

"Would that be the leadership you need from your management team?" The Mystic turned the subject in a new direction.

"Yes it would." Alex nodded in agreement.

"Wouldn't David and Ed need some help and education on leadership? Wouldn't they need to understand your vision and mission?" the Mystic asked.

"That's right," Alex agreed. "They would need some education on the vision and mission. They have to be the ones to explain it to their subordinates."

"Wouldn't you have to let David and Ed know what leadership role you expect them to play?" the Mystic asked.

"Yes. I am counting on them to lead their team," Alex acknowledged.

"So, you need to go over the roles and responsibilities of a manager with David and Ed," the Mystic concluded.

"Now I understand what you mean." Alex lit up as he grasped the understanding of the enormous task ahead.

"Good. To be more specific, if you were to build a sustainable operation, your managers' roles and responsibilities will have to be to..." The Mystic paused, walked up to the white board, and wrote:

Roles and Responsibilities of a Manager
Communicate, educate, inspire, and interact with the people you manage to achieve the results expected of your organization

"By the time you go through this exercise with your management team, you will have begun to establish your authority and leadership role. Also, after you are done, people like David and Ed should have become clearer about their roles and responsibilities. In this respect, you have communicated to them your expectations," the Mystic summarized.

"I think I am getting it." Alex kept his eyes on the white board as he tried to absorb all the information.

"Not only that, your first few meetings will set the tone and direction of your operation. With respect to timing, you must seize the moment if you want to take charge quickly." The Mystic tightened his fist to make his point.

"What I am hearing is that besides recruiting my managers and getting them to buy in to the project, I need to make sure they understand their roles and responsibilities. I need to take advantage of the opportunity to do this in the team formation stage. This way, not only will mutual expectations be clearly communicated, my authority and leadership will be established as well," Alex summarized.

"Alex, I think you have it." The Mystic was happy for Alex and offered him a suggestion. "Now, go do your homework and prepare to bring your team together. Win the respect from each of your managers. Then win the respect from your entire team."

"I have some work to do," Alex agreed appreciatively. "I am glad I talked to you. I need to make my message very easy to understand and clear."

Alex and the Mystic said good-bye. Alex hurried off because he knew he had a lot of preparation to do for tomorrow's meeting with his future managers. That night, Alex stayed up late, taking down notes and practicing his delivery on what he would say.

Alex reflected on the conversation, and entered into his notebook the following:

- Your role changed after your promotion. First you must elevate your level of management and start taking charge.
- If your managers are to be a part of your management team, they will also have much more responsibility.
- Failure to be clear on your managers' roles and responsibilities will rest on you.
- The subject of communication is more involved than most people realize.
- You want to be clear on what and how your managers are going to communicate with you and with their subordinates. You want to lay down the rules of engagement right from the start.
- Managing communication is more involved. Your managers need to be trained on all aspects.
- Educating your managers on communication and leadership will be your responsibility. You should start right away This process empowers you to take charge sooner.
- In order to get everyone on board, you need to

educate all your managers so that they can, in turn, properly educate their subordinates.

- If you are to build a sustainable operation, your managers' roles and responsibilities will have to be clear.

- **Roles and Responsibilities of a Manager**
  Communicate, educate, inspire, and interact with the people you manage to achieve the results expected of your organization

Chapter 6 – Meeting With Your Team

Day 10: 8:30 AM

It had turned out to be a busy week. On and off, Alex had touched base with the Mystic and kept him informed on his progress. Alex had been busy recruiting people like David and interviewing people like Ed along with selecting other members of his management team. Alex also worked with his managers on staffing the rest of the team. Generally, people were excited by the new opportunity to advance their careers and the potential new challenge.

Most of the members of Alex's management team and staff had been with the company for a while, although Alex was able to bring in a few new people from the outside. Outwardly, those who had been with the company all congratulated Alex on his promotion. Behind the scenes, though, not all felt that John had made the right choice by promoting Alex. Most people thought that Alex was an able person and a good guy, but questioned his ability to lead this important project, not to mention his ability to achieve a breakthrough for the company. Some of them even felt that they deserved the promotion more than Alex.

These were the people Alex had to work with. He had to balance the responsibilities of having people on his team with existing domain expertise in the business with having to train some people new to the business. He had to figure out how to balance getting the best from existing relationships with inspiring the unknown and unproven members of his team.

This morning, Alex had called a meeting with his management team. It was his plan to talk to his managers before talking to his entire team as a group.

At around 8:30 AM his managers started to show up. Alex shook hands with everyone and thanked them for joining his team. He made a deliberate effort to circulate and not to focus on David, whom he knew quite well. Generally, the atmosphere was pleasant and business-like.

After everyone was settled into their chairs, Alex opened by introducing people individually and noting their credentials and specialties. At times, Alex used humor to lighten the mood. He knew that he could have let everyone introduce themselves, but he chose to do the introductions himself so those who were being introduced knew that Alex knew them and that he recognized their strengths. Those who were listening and observing also got the message that Alex knew his management team well and that each one was there for a specific reason. In this subtle way, Alex began the process of taking charge.

"By now," Alex began, "you have all heard from either John or me about John's vision for this project. You all have a good idea of our mission. Today, I will touch on how we are going to make it happen. Some of you have worked with me before and will, therefore, have an idea of how I operate.

"For the benefit of everyone, and especially those who haven't worked with me before, let me explain how I manage. It is very simple. I manage by three values. My core philosophy is to create success for everyone. I expect everyone to do the same. My number one value is to make and meet commitments and set challenging goals. I expect that from myself and I expect that from all of you. My number two value is to properly plan, budget, and staff projects. Number three is to pay attention to details and take pride in our work. I expect you and your staff to work according to these values and the Core Philosophy. These values will lead to you success."

"Can you explain?" one of the managers interrupted.

"I will be happy to, but in good time. To get a head start, read the book, *Lateral Approach to Creating Success*. Today there is something even more important to touch on. I want to talk about why you are here. I want to talk about your roles and responsibilities."

"I thought you wanted us to take the ball and run with it," David challenged.

"It is good that you brought this up. Yes, I want all of you to take the ball and run with it, but first you have to know what to do with the ball and where to run it to," cautioned Alex.

"All of you will have specific areas of responsibility related to the project. There are also roles and responsibilities that apply equally to all of you here. This way, we will be consistent and everyone will know what to do." Alex paused. He walked up to the white board and wrote:

Roles and Responsibilities of a Manager
Communicate, educate, inspire, and interact with the people you manage to achieve the results expected of your organization

When Alex finished writing, he turned, pointed to David and said, "David, since you know me well, let's start with you. Your job is to communicate, educate, inspire, and interact with the people you manage to achieve the expected results. What would you communicate?"

David laughed as he responded. "I will tell my team to get off their butts and go to work." Everyone laughed along. Alex laughed also as he responded to David's answer.

"Well, that is one form of communication with your subordinates. Not that I endorse your method, David," Alex smiled. There was more laughter in response to Alex's answer.

"What about communication between you and your boss?" he asked David. "Do you want me to kick your butt also?" There was another burst of laughter.

"I don't know," David answered, a little embarrassed.

"Well, David, you and I communicated well when we worked together before, so it is providing feedback and closing the loop we need to improve on. Wouldn't all of you be more effective if you were getting real-time response and guidance on issues? Wouldn't you want that?" Alex looked around and saw many people nodding their heads.

"That is communication between all of you and me. We will set up some routines and communication mechanisms to do that," Alex added.

"Going back to communication with your subordinates, I just mentioned that I will be managing by values. Do you think your subordinates will understand? Shouldn't they know how we plan to manage?" Alex looked around for responses.

"I know they don't know," one manager said.

"Even if they know, I am not sure they will understand without some assistance," another manager added.

"Even I don't understand!" Another commented, resulting in more laughter.

Alex was prepared to respond.

"I expect you to learn. After you learn, I expect you to communicate and educate your subordinates on our management principles. These will be our rules of engagement. It is important to lay down our principles and rules. Can you do that?" Alex paused and looked around and saw many people nodding.

He continued, "By now, you understand John's vision. Our mission is to execute that vision. You should understand that. But, we cannot expect the rest of our team to understand the full scope and all its implications. It will be your role and responsibility to communicate and educate your subordinates on John's vision, our mission, and expectations. If you don't do this, our people will be working blindly. They will not be successful. One day, they will wake up and find themselves totally lost. Your responsibility is to make sure that won't happen. Any questions so far?" Alex paused to wait for questions. Since there were none, he continued.

"You will find your communication role will include communication with your clients, vendors, alliances, and other operations within our company." Alex paused and looked around to determine his audience's understanding of what he was saying. Then he continued.

"Let's move on to another one of your roles and responsibilities. We have a challenging job ahead of us. It will not be easy. We need our people to walk the extra mile. We need our people to embrace change. This is where your leadership skills come in. I expect you to inspire our people." Alex looked around and noted an elevated level of interest.

"I plan to talk to the entire team as a group very soon. What do you think they would be interested in hearing from me?" he asked.

"I think people will want to know how you plan to lead this project to success," one manger responded.

"They will want to know what you want them to work on to be more effective and cut costs at the same time," another manager said.

"They will want to hear how you can help boost their careers," a third noted.

"I want to know the answers to these questions myself," a fourth admitted.

"I am happy to answer some of these questions. Let's bo frank. I don't have all the answers and it is not important for us to have all the answers at this moment. Our mission is to find the answers. I believe the answers to many of the questions are actually in all of us. My plan is to put our heads together and arrive at a new and better solution, a breakthrough solution. That is why I brought all of you together. Do you think we can do it?" Alex wanted his management team to take ownership of developing the answers, so he put the challenge on his team instead of answering outright.

"Ed, can we do it?" Alex looked at Ed.

"Yes, if we pull together," Ed answered.
"David, how about you?" Alex looked at David.

"You know I do everything and I can do anything," David replied lightheartedly but with confidence.

"How about you?" Alex looked at another manager.

"Yes, we are innovative enough," the manager responded positively.

"Yes, we have a talented group of people here," another agreed.

"Yes, if we can't do it, no one can," came another positive response.

Alex continued to look around. It seemed as if his management team was beginning to understand and respect Alex and his messages.

Alex opened up the meeting for general discussion.

Chapter 7 – Do Something and Do It Fast

Day 10: 12:00 Noon

Alex took a seat near the window of the restaurant so that he could watch out for the Mystic's arrival. He was to meet the Mystic for lunch today and pick his brain further. Alex was happy with the outcome of his first meeting with his managers. He felt that he was building the respect and authority to lead his operation. His excitement built as the minutes ticked away.

When the Mystic arrived, Alex went up to the front of the restaurant to greet him. After they exchanged some small talk and ordered their food, the Mystic began by asking Alex, "How did your meeting go?"

"I believe it went quite well. When I began defining the roles and responsibilities of managers, I almost tripped myself up by asking David for the first response," Alex replied, purposefully being a little mysterious.

"What happened?" the Mystic asked, as Alex had expected.

"David, being David, made a wise crack. He probably thought it was funny. Not that I haven't been guilty of such sins as well," Alex explained.
"So how did you handle the situation?" the Mystic pursued.

"Well, I went along and laughed, but I turned the tables around so we all had some laughs. No harm was done," Alex was happy to explain.

"Good, so what were the end results?" the Mystic asked.

"To begin with, as you expected, most of the managers didn't know the full spectrum of their roles and responsibilities. It was somewhat of an eye opener. I touched on the subject of communication and education then went deeper into the various roles and different aspects of communication, education, and leadership. I gave them time to digest what was said. Now the subject is out in the open for me to revisit as needed," Alex outlined.

The Mystic wanted to know more. "Excellent. So how did your managers respond?"

"Before the meeting, I believe the managers were attracted by the opportunity but weren't all sure I could do the job. It wasn't where I wanted to be, yet I believe the conversation gained me some credibility and respect and that, at the least, there was something they could learn from me during this assignment. After all, people want to experience personal growth as they build their careers, don't they?"

"You are right, Alex," confirmed the Mystic. "So what is your next step?"

As lunch arrived, Alex a took a little time to regroup his thoughts and talk about his plan.

"I plan to talk to all the people in my operation as a group," Alex continued.

"What will you talk to them about?" the Mystic asked, curious.

"I will be talking about John's vision," Alex answered matter-of-factly.

"That's good, what else?" The Mystic wasn't satisfied.

"I will be talking about our goals and our action plan for the next three years," Alex again answered confidently.

"Oh! Your three-year plan? You will be talking about goals and actions that extend into the future longer than I would suggest. Do you think that will build authority and partnerships for you?" the Mystic asked.

Alex was a little confused. "Wouldn't we want our people to know where they are heading and what the path is for getting there?"

"Alex, keep in mind, not everyone can see that far ahead," the Mystic advised. "It may even be confusing since you don't have all the answers yet. Besides, it is not important what you say. It is more important what your team hears, isn't it?"

"That is true. What would be your suggestion?" Alex asked.

"With the opportunity facing you and your team standing ready to do battle, I would suggest you **do something and do it fast**. Nothing beats a quick win and immediate success." With this, the Mystic introduced a new Lateral Approach principle.

"What about the long term?" Alex asked.

The Mystic paused to take a sip of coffee before beginning to explain. "It is more important that you, not necessarily everyone, are clear about what is ahead for the longer term at this time. I am not suggesting that you keep your people in the dark. Don't misunderstand me. If you are to build authority and partnerships, begin by producing results first. If you can capture your people's respect, strengthen your authority, and maintain your partnerships, there will be plenty of opportunities to make longer term goals and plans."

Obviously curious, Alex asked, "What could be the 'something' you want me to do and what do you mean by 'fast'?"

"I cannot tell you what the 'something' is. It gets back to making and meeting commitments and setting challenging goals. I would say, it should be something challenging but not too challenging so that you have a high degree of confidence in achieving success. As an example, say you are the captain of a new battleship and you have to test the ship out to see what its limits are. Can you think of something that fits within these parameters?" the Mystic probed.

"Oh yes, I think there are some important milestones that fit this example. But what is considered fast?" Alex seemed to know what to do, but was still unsure how fast it would have to be accomplished, according to the Mystic.

"You might think that what is considered fast depends on your business and industry, might you? It does not. When you are doing something and doing it fast, in reality you are rallying your team and establishing your credibility, authority, and leadership. You should be able to do that within 30 days. If it takes you longer, you may want to review what's going on, and include what's going on with yourself." The Mystic explained the subtleties.

"Now I understand why you want me to do something and do it fast, but why 30 days and not longer or shorter?" asked Alex, puzzled.

The Mystic explained. "I say 30 days because 90 days would be too long. That is one full reporting period already. On the other end of the spectrum, anything less than 30 days may be too quick to achieve something substantial. You would not have given your people sufficient time to work together or to get to know you. Thirty days is just about the right amount of time to target for taking full charge of the situation," he clarified. "How long you think it will be for your people to react?"

"I think they don't expect the speed aspect," Alex worried.

"So, what will happen?" asked the Mystic.

"They will focus on whether the 30-day goal was achievable?" Alex questioned.

The Mystic agreed, adding, "In other words, the team focus will shift from John's vision, which is further away, to your goals and actions, which are more short term and within grasp. From the team perspective, the risk of not being able to achieve success has now been reduced substantially, hasn't it?"

Alex wanted to make sure he understood. "So by doing something and doing it fast, we refocus the team on short-term goals and actions and reduce the risk of not achieving success. Therefore, the team is more willing to follow my leadership and give me authority."

"You've got it, Alex. Now when you talk to your team, do you know what to do?" the Mystic asked.

"Besides briefly talking about the long term vision and mission, I guess I would spend more time challenging the team to set a 30-day plan for achieving some of our goals. This way, I can rally the entire team and bring the vision closer so it becomes real and within reach." Alex readjusted his thinking to include the Lateral Approach concept of 'Do Something and Do It Fast'. The new message was now quite different from where he had originally planned to start the conversation.

"Very good. Now I am ready for desert," the Mystic smiled and joked.

Alex reflected on the conversation, and he entered into his notebook the following:

Do Something and Do It Fast

- Talking about goals and action plans that are too long term may not help you build authority and partnerships.

- Not everyone can see that far ahead. Talking about a long-term plan may even be confusing since you don't have all the answers yet.

- With the opportunity facing you and your team standing ready, you should **do something and do it fast**. Nothing can beat a quick win and success.

- It is more important that you, not necessarily everyone, are clear about what is in place for the longer term at this time. This does not suggest that you are to keep your people in the dark.

- If you are to build authority and partnerships, begin by producing results first. If you can capture your people's respect, strengthen your authority, and maintain your partnerships, there will be plenty of opportunities to make longer-term goals and plans.

- Doing something and doing it fast is another form of making and meeting commitments and setting challenging goals. It should be something challenging but not too challenging so that you have a high degree of confidence for success. For example, if you are the captain of a new battleship, you have to test the ship out to see what its limits are.

- When you are doing something and doing it fast, in reality you are rallying your team and establishing your credibility, authority, and leadership. You should be able to do that within 30 days. If it takes you longer, you may want to review what's going on, including with yourself.

- Thirty days is the right amount of time because 90 days would be too long. That is one full reporting period already. On the other end of the spectrum, anything less than 30 days may be too quick to do something more substantial. You will not have given your people sufficient time to work together or to get to know you. Thirty days is just about the right amount of time you should target for being fully in charge.

- By doing something and doing it fast, you can refocus the team to short-term goals and actions. From the team perspective, their risk for not succeeding is reduced. Therefore, they are more willing to follow your leadership, giving you the authority.

Day 12: 8:15 AM

It was the morning of the general meeting. Alex took a peek at his watch and went back to reviewing his notes for the last time. Then he closed his folder and did a mental review of the various points he planned to make.

Overall, Alex felt comfortable that he was now well prepared. John, his boss, had been properly briefed. His key managers were aware of the content of his messages. The 30-day objective for completing a pilot program had been well received. Following the Mystic's advice to do something and do it fast, he now knew exactly what to do and how to do it. He was confident that the stage was set for a positive outcome to the meeting. Relaxed, Alex put on his jacket and started walking over to the meeting room.

Most of his staff had arrived early or on time. John was also present and was mingling with the people on the team. John seemed to be in high spirits as he socialized with people and shared old war stories of his experiences as a young executive.

Calling the meeting to order, Alex thanked John for attending and invited him to share his vision with the rest of the team.

When John spoke, he began by praising his audience for their hard work in the past, and provided a brief, positive company outlook. John explained that his expectations moving forward were not about working harder and achieving marginal improvement. John's expectation was for this team to blaze a new trail and lead the way to working smarter and achieving improvement by ten-fold.

John complimented Alex's past achievements and endorsed him as the champion for this transformation project. As John concluded his talk and acknowledged applause from the audience, Alex quietly smiled, now empowered to lead this team.

Alex stood up and humbly accepted the challenge from John. He then turned to his audience and challenged the team to do something and do it fast through the pilot program. He went into detail of the parameters and goals of the pilot program, and thoroughly explained why he believed that their goals were achievable. He instructed his managers and team to properly plan, budget, and staff this project to ensure success. He further explained how the key to a flawless execution is paying attention to details and taking pride in the quality of their work.

As Alex anticipated when he opened up the meeting for questions, most of the questions were meaningful and practical regarding the execution of the pilot program. Alex noted to himself that John's vision was no longer a dream. The vision had now been converted into actionable items and would soon become a reality.

Later on, the feedback Alex received from his managers was mostly very positive. Alex felt that the meeting had taken him another step forward in building his authority and partnerships within his team.

Chapter 8 – Authority Building Exercises

Day 12: 1:00 PM

Alex and the Mystic walked into their favorite lunch place. Because of the late hour, most of the normal lunch crowd had either left or were about ready to leave, making their regular table in a corner by the window a private spot to discuss business.

The Mystic seemed to share Alex's excitement at the progress being made at work. After they ordered their lunch, the Mystic started off with his usual question.

"Well, Alex, how did it go?"

"I basically followed your suggestion to do something and do it quickly," Alex answered.

"So, what did you decide to do quickly?" the Mystic inquired.

Alex was happy to let the Mystic know what he had decided on. "In this case, since we are talking about doing more with less, I chose to start a pilot program. This way, we can test our concept and assumptions and fine tune the business model according to the results," he outlined.

"That sounds like a good idea! What will be the time frame?" the Mystic asked.

"I gave it 30 days from today. It will be a challenge, but it is doable because we can control what the pilot project includes," Alex answered.

"That is true. So how did your people respond?" asked the Mystic.

"Well, it was pretty much what we expected. By the time I spoke, I had already worked with my managers to come to a consensus on what would be included in the 30-day pilot project," Alex answered with confidence.

"In essence, you orchestrated your success," the Mystic confirmed with a smile.

"In essence, yes," Alex answered and smiled back.

With a curious look on his face, the Mystic asked, "What about John? What did he do for you?"

"Through his presence and endorsement, he empowered me to act and manage. That helps a lot," Alex emphasized.

"What else did John say?" the Mystic asked.

"John talked about his vision."

"And you? What did you talk about?" the Mystic continued.

"I talked about the pilot project based on John's vision," Alex answered.

The Mystic wanted to know more. "What was the impact?"

"The combination was quite powerful," Alex shared. "With John talking about his vision, I was able to leverage that vision to rally my people toward it. Had it been my vision instead of John's, I probably would have had to come up with more justification. Instead, I could quickly focus on the pilot project as a very near term reality. I made what we need to do very clear and unambiguous so people wouldn't have to speculate as to what will happen. By doing this, I probably avoided a longer debate later on about what to do or how to do it, and so on, and so on."

"Do you feel you are in a better position to take charge?" the Mystic wanted to know.

"Absolutely! I guess my people, like most people, are looking for someone to lead them to success. With the possibility of a victory within reach, it wasn't so hard to make them believers in the cause," Alex answered.

"Do you think you have completed building your authority and partnerships with your people?"

"Oh yes. I think I am in a good position."

"Now, you just have to make sure it continues to stay that way, don't you?" the Mystic teased.

"That is true, but how do I do that?" Alex asked.

"Have you thought about setting up regular team meetings?" the Mystic suggested.

Alex was somewhat puzzled. "How can regular meetings help?"

The Mystic smiled as he answered. "Regular meetings are meant to control your organization's performance. You know that, don't you? When regular meetings are properly run, they become authority building exercises."

"I thought regular meetings were for information exchange. I sure didn't know that they can be used for building authority," Alex admitted.

"Let me ask you this. Do you have sufficient resources to support all your team's possible needs and goals?" the Mystic asked.

"Of course not," Alex answered.

"In the case of limited resources, wouldn't your responsibility and your authority position you to withhold, grant, or transfer resources from one part of your organization to another?" The Mystic tried to force Alex to think it through from a lateral perspective.

"Yes," he replied, "when such actions are called for."

"Regular meetings are used to evaluate the organization's operations, identify need for change, authorize attention to these needs, approve recommendations for action, and allocate the resources that make the organization's mission a reality," the Mystic explained. "When you carry out your management responsibilities, these meetings are a tool for building and exercising your formal authority."

"I have held regular meetings before, but I didn't realize the implications. I thought of such meetings more in terms of information updates and exchanges. Now I can see that regular meetings provide a platform for authority building." Alex was beginning to understand.

"I believe many people are just like you. They, too, don't realize that regular meetings support authority-building exercises. Therefore, like you, they have either missed opportunities or misused opportunities," the Mystic said.

"What about the information exchange aspect?" Alex asked.

"When it comes to information exchange, isn't it also true that how information is collected, distributed, interpreted, and applied is at the heart of the management function and, therefore, is another means of building authority?" the Mystic challenged.

"What you just said gives me some insight into the dynamics of regular meetings. I used to conduct one-on-one meetings with my managers regularly. Would that be the kind of meeting you are talking about?" Alex asked.

"No," the Mystic quickly corrected. "The classic one-on-one style meetings are powerless."

Surprised by the Mystic's answer, Alex asked why.

115

The Mystic explained further. "It is powerless because if decisions are made by a leader in private, the team remains uninformed. You will find yourself conducting a one-on-one meeting even when others are in the same room. While you are gathering information, those you have not met with will fool that the meeting is irritatingly a waste of time for them. When people are not participating, you can't build authority over them, can you?"

"So, to build authority, it is important for people to participate in regular group meetings, right?" Alex wanted to verify.

"That's it," the Mystic encouraged Alex.

Alex wanted to know more. "What additional advice can you share with me?"

"I may not be able to give you the specifics because the subject can be very broad. What I can tell you is that well prepared meetings that result in action help build respect and authority for the leader. Poorly prepared meetings that result in non-action or indecision will reduce respect and authority for the leader," advised the Mystic.

"What I'm hearing is that meetings should result in actions by the people participating in arriving at those actions. When that happens, it builds respect and authority for the leader," Alex confirmed.

"Alex, I think you have it."

Alex and the Mystic continued talking about the many fine points of improving the effectiveness of authority building exercises over the next two hours. When they were finally done, Alex was excited to try out what he had just learned. He said good-bye to the Mystic and hurried back to his office.

Alex sent out a meeting invitation and an agenda to his managers, inviting them to the first of a new series of regular meetings on the following day. On his way home that night, he visualized the dynamics of tho mccting.

Alex reflected on the conversation, and he entered into his notebook the following:

Authority Building Exercise

- Most people are looking for someone to lead them to success. With a short-term victory that is within reach, it is not so hard to make people believe in the cause.

- Once you have built your authority and partnerships, you just have to make sure it continues to stay that way.

- Regular meetings are meant to control your organization's performance.

- When regular meetings are properly run, they become your authority-building exercises.

  - In the case of limited resources, it is your responsibility and authority to withhold, grant, or transfer resources from one part of your organization to another.

  - Regular meetings are used to evaluate the organization's operation, identify needs for change, authorize attention to these needs, approve recommendations for action, and allocate the resources that will make the organization's mission a reality.

  - When you carry out your management responsibilities, you can use these regular meetings as your tools for building and exercising your formal authority.

- Most people don't realize that regular meetings are authority-building exercises.

- When it comes to information exchange, how information is collected, distributed, interpreted, and employed is at the heart of the management function and, therefore, authority-building.

- Classic one-on-one meetings are powerless because if decisions are made by a leader in private, your people will be uninformed. You will find yourself conducting a one-on-one meeting even though many people are in the same room. Most of the people will feel that the meeting is irritatingly a waste of time for them. When people are not participating, it isn't authority-building.

- Meetings that are well prepared for result in actions that help build respect and authority for the leader. Meetings that are poorly prepared for result in non-action or indecision and will reduce respect and authority for the leader.

Day 13: 8:30 AM

The next day, Alex started the meeting promptly at 8:30 AM. He began by clarifying his expectations and the rules and purpose of this new regular meeting.

"Welcome, everyone. All of you have participated in and run meetings before. I am sure it isn't your favorite pastime. In the spirit of John's vision, I am setting some new rules for what will become regular meetings.

"To start with, they will be more participatory. When you enter this room, you are to leave your title outside. When you participate in these meetings, you are to no longer represent only the interests of your group or section. Instead, I expect you to take on the responsibility of a leader, which means that every aspect of our organization is of your concern. There are no exclusions or exceptions. Anyone can speak out on any subject under discussion.

"In other words, the authority of this meeting is the same as that of a formal leader. You are a part of this leadership." Alex looked around the room. He noticed some people's faces had lighted up. He also saw a couple of people looking a little surprised and puzzled. "If you don't fully understand what I am talking about, I ask you not to worry. It will become clear as our meetings progress," Alex continued.

"Alex, I manage my section, so how can I not represent my section?" one manager asked.

"I expect you to take part in the leadership role. It is very understandable that your expertise may be in your own section of work. But, if your concerns are limited only to representing your section, you won't be a valuable advisor to the leadership role or to the authority this meeting represents, will you?" Alex answered.

"Can we bring up any subject matter even though the subject is not within our line of authority?" another manager asked.

"Absolutely, as long as it is constructive. Let me make it clear that this not a gripe session," Alex emphasized.

121

"This meeting format sounds good to me. I am encouraged. I can already see that these meetings will allow us to collaborate and coordinate better. I feel that we can all contribute to the leadership role and take on the responsibility. It might take us a little time to adjust, but I think we are ready. At least, I am," a third manager confirmed.

Alex took the opportunity to initiate the meeting. "Good! With that, let us begin. Ben, you are responsible for the plan, so why don't you bring us up-to-date on the status of the plan for the pilot project?"

"We are making good progress on putting together the plan. We have one scope-related issue having to do with the free-style design and the resource requirement," Ben summarized.

"Comment from anyone?" Alex asked. No one volunteered.

Alex looked at George and asked, "George, you are our production expert. What are the issues here?"

"Well, the free-style design is the preference from the designer viewpoint. Frankly, it is out of my league to advise you on client preference. I can't tell if the curvature is the fashion. From a production viewpoint, the costs will be significantly higher by as much as 75%. This is because we are on the leading edge of production," George responded.

"Thank you, George. I am no fashion expert either. That honor goes to Linda. Linda, please help us," Alex said, redirecting the question.

"Attention to ergonomics and clean lines are in. To design properly will take a little more time and research. We may run out of time for the pilot. Also, some research is needed to check out pricing. The higher cost of production may drive us to a new price point, which may not be what we are targeting," Linda, the product manager, responded.

Alex asked, "Linda, what can we do to help you get to the bottom of this matter? We don't have the time to do full marketing research."

Ben, the Services manager, suggested, "Someone can talk to a few existing clients and check out their preferences."

"Who has contact with the client?" Alex asked.

"Perhaps someone should contact Steve in Sales," Roy in Engineering interjected.

"Linda, can you do that for us?" Alex suggested.

"Be glad to," Linda replied.

"This will be an action item. Linda will contact Steve in Sales to get a quick read on client preference and pricing. Linda, we don't have much time, so it has to be a quick turnaround, OK? Let's make sure our minutes reflect this action item."
"Got it." Linda was happy to accept. The rest of the team responded with approval, some cheering her on.

"Let's talk about the resource issue," Alex continued. "We gave ourselves the luxury of time on the design issue. We will not have the same luxury regarding resources. We have to be ready the minute we say go. What are our choices?"

Sherman in Implementation was the first to respond.

"Ben, George, and I talked about this resource issue. The resource shortage shifts from Implementation to Engineering or from Engineering to Implementation depending on our approach. We couldn't quite figure it out," he said.

"Are you saying that even if production winds up taking more time, the benefit will be easier implementation and, therefore, require less implementation resources? And vise versa that if we produce faster, the trade-off is that implementation will require more resources?" Alex asked.

"Those are the issues," Sherman answered.

"So, what will it take to figure it out?" Alex asked

"Of course, my preference is to have a faster and easier implementation," Sherman replied. "You are not just saying that because you represent Implementation, are you?" Alex wanted to know.

"No," Sherman answered.

"Then what are you basing your recommendation on?" Alex asked.

"The fact that each implementation will cost the company more," Sherman reasoned.

"How do you know?" Alex challenged. "How do you know it will cost the company more, if production costs are also higher?"

"From that perspective, I don't know," Sherman admitted.

Alex switched his attention to another source. "George, can I get some advice from you?"

"I guess we cannot resolve this without determining the final bottom line. Perhaps the result of the pilot project will give us a definite answer," George suggested.

Sherman concurred, thinking now at the organizational level. "That might not be a bad idea. We might begin by sharpening our pencils and looking at the figures. From there, we should be able to make a decision based on our best judgment. If it proves out through the pilot project, then we have confirmation of our decision."

"It seems like we have a good solution and a couple of action items. Sherman, why don't you work with George to go through the numbers? Report back on your recommendations and the assumptions you are using. George, why don't you work with Accounting to track the costs of this pilot project for the purpose we mentioned. Keep our timeline in mind. Let the minutes reflect these two actions. Any questions?" Alex looked around. He found Sherman and George nodding their heads, busy taking down notes for their action items.

As the meeting progressed, Alex felt more and more in control. The meeting quickly fell into a routine of presentation on the issues, discussion, decision, and commissioning people for action items. His managers also were quickly getting accustomed to the process as they went down the list of items on the agenda. It became obvious that Alex was in charge. At the same time, his people felt empowered.

Chapter 9 – Make Friends and Influence Actions

Day 20: 1:00 AM

Alex was again having lunch with the Mystic. It was becoming a regular thing as both Alex and the Mystic were enjoying each other's company and the exchange of ideas. Today, the Mystic noticed something was bothering Alex.

He asked, "What is on your mind, Alex?"

"Something Linda told me this morning and the problem she is encountering that is slowing our project down," Alex explained.

"What did she tell you?" the Mystic asked, concerned.

"I commissioned Linda to work with Sales to get feedback from our clients. It appears the people in Sales weren't as responsive as we needed," Alex explained.

"I see. Linda is encountering problems driving people across the line of authority, is that so?" The Mystic leaned back and smiled as he inquired.

"Yes, and I don't quite know what to do." Alex noticed that the Mystic seemed to already have an answer and he hoped for a solution.

"Of course you do, don't you?" the Mystic encouraged.

"But I don't want to make the situation worse by going over people's heads." Misinterpreting the Mystic's anticipated suggestion, Alex was concerned.

"Who said you have to? As far as going over other people's heads, it all depends on how you initiate the contact," the Mystic quickly clarified.

"So, how would you handle the situation?" Alex asked.

"Make friends. Then you can influence actions." The Mystic introduced a new Lateral Approach concept.

Over the rest of the lunch, Alex and the Mystic had a very long conversation. As the Mystic spoke, Alex nodded his head until, finally, his face lit up. Saying good-bye to the Mystic, it was obvious he was happy and ready for action.

Back at his office, Alex requested that Linda join him. Alex was obviously delighted when Linda walked in. Linda, on the other hand, was not in the best of moods. She was concerned that she couldn't meet the timeline and was delaying the rest of the team.

Alex responded to the situation. "Linda, this is not your best day, is it? Why don't you tell me about it?"

Linda expressed her concerns. "More than a week has passed and we only have feedback from one client. That is as good as not having any. We cannot make decisions based on one client's feedback. We don't have that much time left. I met with Sales again today. Steve assigned Tony to work with me. He didn't have anything new for me, again. I can't count on him. Probably tomorrow will be the same. I am getting very worried. I don't think Sales really wants to help us."

"Linda, I know that you are very worried and frustrated and that you want to do well for the team. I think Sales also has good intentions and wants to help." Alex wanted to take the high road in approaching the situation.

"Alex, I am not so sure." Linda had her doubts.

"You got at least one customer's feedback, didn't you? Better than none, so we are still ahead," Alex pointed out positively.
"What can we do with just one?" Linda saw the glass as half empty.

"Look, Linda, we must think very positively. Sales isn't within our line of authority. But, if we want to make friends and influence their actions, we need to appeal to their nobler side. To us, eight days is a long time. To them, it is a short time. We need to try to understand it from their point of view." Alex began to redirect Linda's thinking to a Lateral Approach.

Puzzled, Linda asked, "How can we make friends and influence actions as you said?"

"That is what I intend to help you with." Alex said, and that was just what Linda wanted to hear.

"That would be great! I can use some help. You may be able to twist some arms and tell Tony what to do," Linda responded with obvious delight.

"That isn't my intention at all," Alex corrected her. "Because that would not help you in the longer term. Here is something you can do to help yourself."

"What's that?" Linda asked.

"Why don't you write me a few notes about what you and Tony have done and accomplished and what you plan to do, in one page or less. Make sure it is factual and make sure it is positive. I am not asking you to put your complaint in writing," Alex instructed.

"Why one page or less? Why so specific?" Linda asked, still puzzled.

"While you are writing to me, your audience is really Steve. If your audience is an executive, your message has to be at the appropriate executive level. In this case, one page or less will do the job," Alex explained.

"What then?" Now Linda was more curious.

"I will go make some friends for us. I plan to invite you and Tony to the meeting," Alex replied, explaining to Linda what he planned to do next.

"It is important to hear from you the positive things that Tony has done for us," Alex began.

"What? He hasn't done nearly enough. Besides, how would that help?" Linda found Alex's instructions not so easy to do.

"You will see how far you can go by appealing to others' nobler side," Alex encouraged.

"Well, I will follow your advice, but I wouldn't bet my money on it turning out well," Linda agreed somewhat reluctantly.

"Before you form your judgment, why don't you wait? I am going to call Steve and see if I can catch him." Alex deliberately remained mysterious about what he had planned. He knew that Linda would not be convinced by words. He knew that she would only be convinced by seeing it in action and with positive results.

Alex dialed Steve's extension and was relieved to get a hold of him on the first try.

"Steve speaking."

"Hi Steve, this is Alex. Is this my lucky day or what? Getting a hold of a busy guy like you on my first try! How are you?" Alex exchanged pleasantries with Steve.

135

"Very good, thank you," Steve answered, adding, "By the way, congratulations on your promotion! I heard that you have a new and important initiative."

"That's why I'm calling. Linda and Tony are doing some work together for the project and need your help. I will be over in your area tomorrow; would we be able to spend a few minutes together so we can update you? Probably 15 to 20 minutes will do." Alex asked for a short meeting realizing that it would be hard for Steve to refuse.

"Sure. I do have quite a few meetings tomorrow, but if all you need is 15 minutes, I can squeeze that in," Steve accepted.

"It will probably be around 11:00 or so. I will be with Linda, and would you ask Tony to join us?" Alex set up the meeting participants.

"Sounds good, 11:00 it is. See you tomorrow," Steve acknowledged.

After Alex hung up the phone, he turned to Linda.

"Linda, we're on. Get me that one page report and see you at 11:00 at Steve's office. Here is what I expect to be on the report." Alex gave Linda a few pointers. Before she left, Alex smiled and gave her a thumbs-up sign. Linda smiled back. She wasn't exactly sure what was going to happen, but she felt more relieved. After all, she was getting the attention and help she needed.

Day 21: 11:00 AM

The next morning, Alex and Linda arrived at Steve's office promptly at the appointed time. They quickly shook hands and exchanged some small talk. Alex began by thanking Steve for his support and interest in the new initiative.

"Steve, I know that you have a busy day. Let me get down to business. John asked me to head this new operation and to explore ways to do things smarter and faster; doing more with less. We have a pilot project with a very tight deadline as our starting point. That is why Linda approached you to get Tony to help us get some feedback from our clients." Alex paused and looked at Steve for acknowledgement.

"Yes, Linda mentioned that to me," he confirmed.

At this point, Alex looked at Linda and signaled for her to hand Steve her one page report. As soon as Linda handed it over, Alex continued.

Date

To: Tony, Sales Representative
From: Linda, Design Specialist, Tower Project
Cc: Alex, Director, Tower Project
Re: Progress Report

Our attempt to obtain an initial product design response has a good start. Here is what we have accomplished.

- Purposes and goals communicated
- Up to ten targeted clients identified
- To-date, one client responded. Tony's effort is appreciated.

For the next weeks, my plan is to simplify the form and questions for the clients. Tony will be requested to do the follow-up.

The pilot project is on a tight deadline. Knowing Tony also has other commitments related to his regular work, his extra effort is much appreciated.

"Let me quickly go through the few bullet points Linda has identified in this report. First of all, thank you, Linda, and thank you, Tony." As Alex mentioned Tony's name, he simultaneously gave him a thumbs-up sign and a smile.

Continuing, Alex noticed that Tony responded with a smile in return.

"We are working on a short time frame, and it seems like we are off to a good start. Linda and Tony, both of you are clear on what you want to accomplish, is that correct?" Alex looked at Tony for confirmation.

"Yes, I am quite clear what Linda wants," Tony confirmed.

"...And both of you identified approximately 10 target clients to get feedback from, is that also correct?" Alex continued.

"That is correct," Tony confirmed again.

"...And one client has already responded. That's good. Good job, Tony," praised Alex.

"Thank you." Tony acknowledged the compliment.

"Since we don't have that much time left, it makes sense to spend only another week on this. According to Linda's plan, she is going to make it easier for the clients to respond. Do you think we can pull this off?" Alex looked at Linda and then looked at Tony.

Tony seemed a little hesitant. He glanced at Steve, as did Alex.

"Tony, go ahead and let Alex and Linda know what is it that you can or cannot do," Steve prompted.

"What I can do is to follow up with these clients," Tony answered.

"If I were to come along, do you think that it would help?" Linda offered.

"It might," Tony replied.

"Well then, why don't you two work as a team in the field," Alex suggested, looking for confirmation from Steve.

"That is a good idea. This way, Linda can help Tony explain to the client what this all about and save some time for Tony and the client," Steve agreed.

"That sounds good," Tony added.

"So we all agree. Thank you very much, Steve."
"Thank you very much, Steve," Linda added.

"By the way, Steve, would you like us to keep you informed on how it's going? At the least, we could copy the report to you, also," Alex said, taking an opportunity to create a communication pipeline.

"That will be fine." As expected, Steve was happy with the offer to be kept in the loop.

"In that case, I won't take up any more of your time." Alex stood up, shook hands and said good-bye. Everyone else did the same.

As soon as Linda and Alex walked out of Steve's office, Linda expressed her delight at the result of the meeting.

"Thank you very much for your help, Alex. What really happened in there?" Linda was excited by the result as well as extremely curious.

"What do you want to know?" Alex asked.

"First of all, why the report routine? Either you or I could have explained the status in a few minutes. From what I can see, the report didn't seem to add anything," Linda noted.

"But it did, Linda. The report added a lot. Don't judge its value by its number of pages. Without saying a word, the message to Steve was that we are organized and we can move fast. The report also gave me an opportunity to give Tony a thumbs-up. Did you notice how he reacted?"

"Yes, I think he appreciated that, especially in front of his boss." Linda was beginning to understand.

"You've got it. The thumbs-up was probably the most important action on our part in the whole meeting," Alex emphasized.

"Really? What did it do?" Linda asked, somewhat surprised.

"The silent message is two-fold. The first message is that we have access to Tony's boss. The second message is that, this time, we were praising him. But he knows very well that it may not always be that way. Moving forward, Tony will be looking to us to provide positive feedback to Steve."

He continued, "That brings to us the influence and, indirectly, the authority over this situation. In a way, this approach makes a direct line of authority unnecessary." Alex began to peel away the not-so-obvious parts of his lateral thinking and approach.

"Wow," Linda replied. "I didn't realize the implications, but it makes sense."

"The report also led us in a leadership exercise," Alex said, peeling off another layer of understanding.

"What leadership exercise?" Linda was surprised again.

"The exercise we performed when we looked ahead and called for action," Alex explained.

"What does the exercise do?" Linda asked.

"The meeting would have become powerless unless it resulted in some kind of action, which it did. Looking ahead and calling for action is a leadership role. When Steve endorsed our solution and signaled Tony to go along with it, he passed the leadership role to us," Alex explained.

"Where do we go from here?" Linda asked.

"What we need to do is to take this leadership role and act and behave like leaders. Keep in mind: we don't have a direct line of authority. We are not Tony's boss. We can only lead and command if people respect us and want to follow us. Understand?" With patience, Alex guided Linda to think laterally.

"I have it. Thank you, I believe I learned a lot today." Finally, Linda understood the messages and saw the solution. Each of Alex's actions made so much sense and was so obviously simple.

"You're welcome. Be sure to keep me informed. Also be sure to keep Steve informed," he reminded her.

Chapter 10 – Doing the Right Thing

Day 24: 11:00 AM

Over the weekend, Alex had not been able to get his mind off work. He ended up not resting well, which added to his frustration. As Alex mentally reviewed his progress to-date step by step, it seemed as if every key initiative was not turning out according to plan. It was not as if his people were not charging ahead or were demonstrating a lack of dedication. It was not as if people were executing incorrectly. They just couldn't deliver the expected results. It seemed like each item needed his personal involvement. As a result, each task was taking longer and costing more than called out in the original plan.

Then there were the road bumps, the unexpected items that were occurring more frequently than they should. At this point, Alex could not visualize the project meeting schedule. He knew that he had to do something about the situation, but he was at loss as to what it was he should be doing.

That was the reason he had scheduled this morning's meeting with the Mystic.

As Alex walked into the Mystic's office, the Mystic took one look at him and knew immediately that Alex was really troubled this time.

"What is the matter, Alex? You don't look like yourself," the Mystic commented.

Alex threw up his hands and said, "Everything seems to be going wrong. The pilot is supposed to establish the processes and methodology we can scale to do more with less. At this point, we seem to be going around in circles. Instead of providing us a road map on how we can improve, we seem to be proving that we cannot do any better than what we have been doing in the past. This is very troubling." Alex's frustration was clearly showing.

"Calm down. It isn't the end of the world. Give me the details," the Mystic encouraged.

"It seems like everything needs my personal attention. Otherwise, the task won't move forward and the problem stays unresolved," explained Alex.

"Yes, what else?" The Mystic tried to get Alex to open up.

"Even after I provide a solution, there are still more road bumps," Alex explained.

"Yes, what else?"

"Then there is the schedule. It seems like people just can't meet the schedule," Alex continued.

"So, what do you think is the problem?" the Mystic asked calmly.

"I am not sure. That is why I am here," said Alex, reaching out for help.

The Mystic tried to help Alex think laterally. "Do you think your people are not capable enough?"

"No, they are the best we have."

"Do you think your objective is too far-reaching?"

"No," Alex relied. "Anything less would only prove that we have no room for improvement. That cannot be the case."

"Do you think your schedule is overly aggressive?" the Mystic asked.

"It is possible, but it is much more than that. There are these road bumps," Alex answered.

"Alex, it seems like you are scratching your head wondering what went wrong. Have you considered if your direction was correct in the first place? Have you considered if the pilot or the way the pilot is being conducted was the right thing to do in the first place? Have you considered whether the premises you are trying to prove needed proving?" Finally, the Mystic felt that the moment had arrived to share another important message with Alex.

"Those are things I have not considered: whether we are doing the right things or doing things right. How can I determine what is the right thing to do?" As he asked these questions, it was as if a light bulb went up over Alex's head. He suddenly realized that there was a lateral approach to thinking this through that he hadn't pursued.

Noticing the change in Alex, the Mystic was encouraged and extended his lateral concept further. "There are times to lead and there are times to listen. Leverage the combined strength and talent of your team. Ask for suggestions."

"What will my team think? Wouldn't that damage my credibility? Will they follow my leadership afterwards?" Alex was concerned.

"Let me put it this way," the Mystic answered. "They certainly will not follow your leadership if you insist on going the wrong direction. Would you?"

"No, I wouldn't," Alex agreed.

"You are trying to break new ground. Everyone recognizes that there are risks involved. As a leader, you have to know when to advance as well as when to retreat. If the pilot project isn't working, everyone on your team has to answer for it. By listening to your managers, not only are you leveraging their expertise, you are getting further buy-in and commitment from them. If you execute this correctly, you will gain authority and respect, not the other way around," the Mystic explained emphatically.

"That's it. I think I will try to do just that." Alex was happy to understand that the situation was not as hopeless as he had thought.

The Mystic gave Alex further encouragement. "By the way, listening to your managers and changing course does not mean the pilot project is a total waste. You just tested a premise that didn't work in order to find one that will."

"You are right." Alex was his old self again. He was excited and ready to get back at it!

"Remember to talk to your boss," the Mystic reminded him. "It is OK. Better to have this happen earlier rather than later. Also listen to his advice."

Back at work, Alex set up meetings for the next day with his managers and John. That night, he once again couldn't fall asleep. This time, though, it wasn't because he was disturbed. He couldn't fall asleep because he was so excited and there was so much more to think about.

What the Mystic had said seemed to have lifted a big load off his shoulders. It wasn't as if all his problems had disappeared. But attacking the underlying direction of the project opened up completely new possibilities for it. Now new ideas were starting to form in his mind. A couple of times, he actually got up out of his bed and wrote down these new ideas.

DAY 25: 8:00 AM

The next morning, Alex made himself a strong cup of coffee and ate a healthy breakfast before he set off for the meeting.

As his managers showed up one-by-one, Alex greeted them enthusiastically. He smiled broadly as he noticed that his managers looked confused, disturbed, and defeated like he had when he went into the Mystic's office yesterday. Alex realized that his managers were probably bracing for a reprimand for failing to meet the target milestone and schedule.

Alex began by saying enthusiastically, "I feel great today although I only got four hours of sleep. How are you all feeling?" This seemed to catch everyone by surprise. Alex's enthusiasm seemed to make his managers a little more relaxed, so he quickly continued.

"I have been keeping up-to-date with the progress of the pilot project. It isn't going the way I originally envisioned. I came to that conclusion after noticing that Patrick over there probably only got four hours of sleep for the whole week. Is that so, Patrick?" The team turned their heads toward Patrick and laughed softly.

"Yes, I do know that all of you have given your full effort in an attempt to pull the pilot project through. I now question some of our underlying assumptions and am evaluating our direction. I asked all of you here today to thank you for your gallant effort and to listen to your suggestions and recommendations. After all, being on the front line, you must have learned a lot about what to do and what not to do." As Alex spoke, the dark cloud in the room seemed to lift a little. A few people even smiled.

One of them spoke out. "When I went to our client to get feedback on some of our ideas for features, they actually gave us many more ideas than what were included in our pilot. They gave me product ideas and services ideas that we can charge for, also."

A second spoke up. "When we look into our current product, we believe that with some modifications, it can compete in a ripe and untapped market segment we have not considered. But entering into a new market segment wasn't a part of our pilot project."

Then a third spoke up. "We know that we can fine tune the product so installation and implementation can be much faster and at a lower cost. Our pilot schedule cannot accommodate the change. Revisiting our underlying premise of the pilot is definitely the right thing to do."

The meeting had gotten off to a good start and lasted for over two hours. New ideas continued to pour out. Alex assigned someone to take notes and capture action items. By the end of the meeting, the team had arrived at a new plan. Alex summarized the new action plan, established a new milestone on progress, and closed the meeting.

With a new solution in hand, Alex felt ready to meet with John. Without delay or an appointment, he arrived at John's office. Fortunately, John was available.

"This is a surprise, Alex! What's up?" John asked, not knowing what to anticipate.

"Sorry for just popping in. I feel it is important that you know what we are doing about the pilot program for the Tower Project." Alex got right to business.

"So what is it?" John asked anxiously.

"Over the last few weeks, my people worked extra hard. None-the-less, they continued to encounter resistance and road bumps. I was wondering if giving the team a little more time would be helpful or not. For us to transform our way of doing business, doing more with less, I came to the conclusion that we weren't going in the right direction. At this point, I feel that it is better to cut our losses and regroup quickly."

Alex continued, "This morning, I gathered my staff and listened very carefully to their findings. They have many excellent suggestions. I want to let you know that I am making a pretty drastic course correction."

Alex began to explain his new action plan and the changes he wanted to make. John listened, emphatically nodding his head as he did and asking questions for clarification. At the end, John spoke.

"Well, Alex, I am glad you decided on the action you are taking. That is what I am counting on you to do. At least you have determined what we should *not* be doing. So what will the impact be to the schedule?" John encouraged.

"In the bigger perspective, the impact should be minimal. Consider this as an investment for a higher rate of returns. I will keep you posted as we proceed. Would that be acceptable?" Alex explained and assured John.

"Go ahead, Alex. Just keep me posted. I am counting on you." John nodded his head and gave Alex a smile.

Alex left John's office feeling confident that he would be able to bring good news the next time he met with John. After all, the new action plan was put together from the field experience of his staff. They were driven to make it work. This time around, it was their plan. They knew that they owned it!

Alex reflected on the conversation, and he entered into his notebook the following:

Doing The Right Thing

- Sometimes things go wrong. When you are wondering what went wrong, don't just consider whether things have been done right or wrong, consider if those things were going in the right direction and were the right things to do in the first place.

- There are times to lead and there are times to listen. Leverage the combined strength and talent of your team. Ask for suggestions.

- With respect to whether asking for suggestions or changing direction would be damaging to your credibility or leadership, lateral thinking is that your people certainly will not follow your leadership if you insist on going in the wrong direction.

- If you are trying to break new ground, everyone recognizes that there are risks involved. As a leader, you have to know when to advance as well as when to retreat.

- If the project isn't working, everyone on your team has a part in it. By listening to your managers, not only are you leveraging their talents and findings, you are getting further buy-in and commitment. If you execute this correctly, you will gain authority and respect.

- Listening to your manager and changing course does not mean the project is a total waste. You just tested a premise that didn't work in order to find one that does.

- When things are not going your way, it is better to inform your boss earlier rather than later. Also listen to your boss's advice.

Chapter 11 – Delegate, Not Abdicate

Day 26: 11:00 AM

The next morning, Alex felt energized. He felt that yesterday had been the turning point for the Tower Project. He was satisfied with the new plan. There were many identifiable innovations. The process made business sense. It was no longer a plan on paper. It was a real plan, executable by real and enthusiastic professionals. It was a breakthrough and Alex couldn't wait to share this new development with the Mystic.

As Alex walked up to their favorite table in their favorite restaurant, the Mystic felt that something had changed. He greeted Alex with a smile and asked, "Well, tell me the good news. You seem happy today!"

Alex complied enthusiastically. "I believe the Tower Project will be successful. My team has had a breakthrough. They put together a new plan that is challenging and I think it will work. I don't have to do much. I just empowered the

161

team. I think I can sit back and let my managers carry the ball."

"Alex, that sounds good. I am happy for you." The Mystic gave Alex a smile and took a sip of coffee.

Alex got the feeling that the Mystic had stopped short with his thoughts and encouraged him to say what was on his mind.

"Well, Alex," the Mystic replied. "Your slower than expected progress and the high expectations of the project put a strain on you. Now, seeing and hearing how you have boosted your managers' morale is indeed encouraging.

"On the other hand," he continued with a small smile, "I have never seen a plan that doesn't look as good on paper as it sounds."

"What do you mean?" Alex was a little perplexed.

"It means that while it is good to empower your people and it is the right thing to do, you must remember that the ultimate responsibility rests on you. You can delegate and you should. But you must not end up abdicating your role and responsibilities. It is a common trap that is very easy to fall into," the Mystic cautioned.

"What do you mean that abdicating is a common trap?" Alex tried to keep up with the Mystic's thinking.

"Empowerment and delegation are necessary management tools for scaling an organization. But, keep this in mind: Your boss selected you and assigned you to head the organization and project. It is your responsibility to make this project successful. Your boss entrusted you because of your vision, ability, and judgment. Until you are released from that responsibility, the bucks stop with you. You are it! Do you understand what I mean?" The Mystic paused and looked hard at Alex.

"I know that it is my responsibility. I am not sure what exactly you are trying to tell me. I thought I was supposed to empower my team and let them do their work. Should I be doing more?" Alex asked.

With sensitivity for Alex's feelings, the Mystic explained, "I am just being cautious. I am not talking about micro-management or saying that you have to come up with every idea or put together every plan."

"Then what are talking about?" Alex asked.

"Your job is to gather the smartest, most able, and most appropriate people for your team. You are to leverage, motivate, and utilize your human resources to the max. That includes using their ideas, creativity, skills, hard work, etc. That is your job," the Mystic reassured Alex.

"Yes, that is what I thought I was doing," Alex insisted.

"The common mistakes a lot of leaders make are to lose sight unknowingly of their responsibility, let loose of their authority, and overlook the importance of regular communication in the name of everyone being too busy." The Mystic steered the conversation back to lateral thinking.

"I agree. How can I prevent making this mistake?" Alex asked impatiently.

"You must not neglect to check and cross check information reported to you and the performance and results of the team," the Mystic instructed.

"What will happen if I don't?" Alex asked.

"If you don't, it won't be long until you are no longer sufficiently knowledgeable about what is really going on to make decisions, evaluate, or judge the actual status of the situation in order to be an effective leader," the Mystic cautioned. "The situation will spiral downward as more time passes. One day, you will wake up with a crisis on your hands. Only at that time will you discover all the missteps, errors, or wrong things that had been going on."

"That won't happen to me," Alex insisted.
"Alex, this may sound strange, but authority is given up through attrition. It won't happen overnight and by design. Normally, abdication creeps in silently. Even experienced leaders

often make this simple mistake," the Mystic explained.

"Let me understand what you are saying," Alex wanted to confirm. "While I am to use the ideas, creativity, skills, and hard work of my staff, I am to maintain my authority through regular communication: by checking and cross checking information and monitoring progress and performance. This is because it is my responsibility and obligation to my assignment and to my boss.

"But I have to ask, does this conflict with making sure people feel ownership of their assignments and jobs?" he asked.

"I am not asking you to become a control freak!" the Mystic responded with a smile. "On the contrary, you want each and every one on your team feeling ownership of their part of the project as well as the project as a whole. Ownership makes people feel responsible and rewarded through their accomplishments."

"I fully agree with you." Alex was glad that the Mystic was telling him something he already knew.

"How about you?" the Mystic asked.

"Me, what about me?" The Mystic's question caught Alex by surprise.

"You, of all people, must also feel ownership of everything, above all the well being of your people and the project." The Mystic led Alex toward another lateral thought.

"What will that do?" asked Alex, unsure of where the Mystic was heading.

"Practicing my suggestion to maintain authority through communication and by checking and cross checking on progress and performance gives you a forum and many opportunities to reinforce the ownership of your team. It gives your people the opportunity to be recognized so that they can take pride in their work. It allows you the opportunity to take the lead and steer your people away from potential problems, missteps, or errors and, therefore, saves you from having to implement corrective actions or give reprimands." The Mystic explained the impact on Alex's authority of taking a Lateral Approach.

Alex's face brightened as the message now became clearer to him. "I think I have it! Had you not mentioned the potential traps to me, I would have been inclined to be less vigilant on exerting my authority. By taking a hands-off approach more than I should, I would not have been able to leverage ownership as much as I could. There seems to be a great balancing act here, isn't there?"

"Alex, it is always a balancing act when it comes to well rounded management." The Mystic sat back and took a long sip of his coffee.

Alex did the same. His mind was already projecting to the next meeting with his managers. He silently thanked his luck that the Mystic had given him these words of caution. Alex felt that he could have easily fallen into a trap had he not had this talk with the Mystic.

Now he was alert and ready to act on his authority.

Alex reflected on the conversation, and he entered into his notebook the following: DP notes:

Delegate, Not Abdicate

- Seeing and hearing your manager getting a boost in morale is indeed encouraging. On the other hand, you will never see a plan that doesn't also look good on paper.

- While it is good to empower your people and it is the right thing to do, you must remember the ultimate responsibility rests on you.

- You can delegate and you should. You must not end up abdicating your role and responsibilities, which you shouldn't. It is a common trap that is very easy to fall into.

- Your boss selected you and assigned you to head the organization and project. It is your responsibility to make this project successful. Your boss trusted your vision, ability, and judgment. Until you are released from that responsibility, the buck stops at your desk. You are it!

- Your job is to gather the smartest, most able and most appropriate people on your team. You are to leverage, motivate and utilize your human resources to the max. That includes using their ideas, creativity, skills, hard work, etc. That is your job.

- The common mistake a lot of leaders make is to lose sight of this responsibility and let loose of their authority and overlook the importance of regular communication in the name of everyone being too busy.

- You must not neglect to check and cross check the information reported, along with the performance and results of the team.

- If you don't have regular communication, it won't take long before you are no longer sufficiently knowledgeable about what is really going on, and you will be unable to make decisions, evaluate or judge the actual status of the situation, and be a good leader. The situation will spiral downward as more time passes. One day, you will wake up with a crisis on your hands as you discover all the missteps, errors or mistakes.

- Authority is given up through attrition. It won't happen overnight or by design. Normally, abdication creeps in silently. Even experienced leaders often make this simple mistake.

- You want each and every one on your team to feel ownership for their part of the project as well as for the project as a whole. Ownership makes people feel responsible and rewarded through their accomplishments.

- You, of all people, must also feel ownership of everything and the well being of your people and the project above all.
- Practicing the Lateral Approach to maintaining authority through communication, checking and cross checking on progress and performance gives you a forum and many opportunities to reinforce the ownership of your team. It gives your people the opportunity to be recognized so that they can take pride in their work. It allows you the opportunity to take the lead and steer your people away from potential problems, missteps, or errors and, therefore, prevent having to determine corrective actions or give reprimands.

Chapter 12 – The Power of Success

Day 45: 10:00 AM

Alex was in the conference room. He checked the projector and presentation for the third time. His managers and staff were scattered around the room. Small groups gathered making small talk. A few had taken up seats. John walked in, looked around and spotted Alex, and walked over to shake his hand.

"How's it going? I can't wait to hear this presentation," John said eagerly. "Shall we get started?"

"Yes, let's go." Alex's enthusiasm began to overcome his nervousness. He knew that he had a good story to tell. His team had finally achieved a breakthrough. He felt especially proud that his team had made it happen. Alex walked to the front of the room and brought the meeting to order, and instantly, the room became quiet.

Alex began by thanking John for giving this team the opportunity and the challenge. He thanked the team for their dedication and creativity. Alex proceeded to introduce his managers one-by-one and give special details on their individual contributions and accomplishments. There was some spontaneous cheering. The positive vibration echoed in the room.

Alex proceeded to qualify their success.

"John, today I am glad to be able to give you a positive report. As you know, we had a false start and hit a few bumps along the way. None-the-less, we were able to achieve breakthroughs in several areas of our operation. I am happy to report that the mission to transform the way we do business has been proven in the field and we have excellent customer acceptance. I am confident that today's success points the way to a successful future. This is just a start."

"Alex, it sounds like you are off to a great start. What I asked of this group – to do more with less – isn't exactly easy or straightforward. I am not too surprised that you encountered some bumps along the way. More importantly, you got to where I wanted you to be. Now let me hear some details and metrics." John's words of encouragement to Alex set the tone for the rest of the meeting.

John began drilling down with a series of in-depth and intense questions. Alex let his managers answer most of the questions, and they were happy to oblige. They liked talking about their own success stories. They ran through their well-prepared presentations, with Alex adding additional insights from the senior management perspective. Where there were opportunities, Alex gave credit to the appropriate people. The atmosphere was dynamic. By the end of the meeting, John was totally convinced and confident that the findings and breakthroughs were significant for the future of the company.

Once again, John expressed his thanks and congratulated the entire team. He shook hands with Alex and purposefully asked him aloud, "Why don't you stop by my office later? I want to talk to you about the next step."

After John left the room, Alex turned toward his staff and gave them a thumbs-up. "Great job!" he said and spontaneously gave a high-five to the manager closest to him, which started a chain of high-fives around the room.

Day 45: 3:00 PM

Alex wanted very much to buy the Mystic lunch as a token of his thanks, but he only had time for coffee. Alex was feeling good about the state of things. He felt as if he could meet any challenge with his team. He felt the mutual respect and appreciation of the team and by the team. He felt in charge and he felt more comfortable leading the next phase.

The Mystic sensed Alex's good mood. "Something very special must be going on for you to want to buy me lunch!" the Mystic teased him.

"Well, we presented our results to John and he was happy, so I am happy." Alex was frank about his feelings.

"What about your managers and your team?" the Mystic inquired.

"They are happy, too. They feel good about their accomplishments," relied Alex happily.

"That's good. So, is the project done?" the Mystic asked.

"No, it is the start of something bigger. John and I already met about the next phase," Alex answered.

"Are you ready?" the Mystic asked.

"As ready as can be! I feel more confident. I feel I can lead. I feel in control." Alex's enthusiasm was obvious.

"That's wonderful. That's the power of success," the Mystic stated.

"Yes, the power of success!" Alex repeated.

"Of course, you may not have been so fortunate if your project had dragged on without positive results," the Mystic reminded.

Alex nodded in agreement with the Mystic. "I know. Doubts were starting to set in with my managers and staff. I adjusted our goal by making our success incremental. Although John didn't say anything, I think he knew what I was facing and, therefore, he accepted the result and celebrated with us."

"I think John is a very smart boss," said the Mystic, leading Alex to a lateral thought. "He understood that if he wanted you to run the project and be in charge, you needed that success. Now your team will follow you."

"I have to thank John the next time I meet with him." It dawned on Alex exactly what had transpired over the past few weeks. Now he knew what to do.

"By the way," the Mystic added with a smile, "if you want to be in charge, you must create success. That means it is time to review *Lateral Approach to Creating Success*.

"Good reminder," Alex smiled and agreed.

About the Authors

Ho-Wing Sit is the author of *Lateral Approach to Creating Success: Simple Principles for Not Leaving Success to Chance Whether You Manage a Small Shop or a Million Dollar Corporation, Lateral Approach to Managing Projects: Simple Principles for Achieving High Customer Satisfaction and Mutual Profitability*, and *Lateral Approach to Taking Charge: Simple Principles for New Bosses on Building Authority and Partnerships*.

Mr. Sit has been pursuing, refining, and applying powerful and effective management principles and techniques for over 30 years. In this third book in the Lateral Approach series, *The Lateral Approach to Taking Charge*, he offers important insights on management vs. leadership and why knowing the difference can empower new managers to meet any challenge.

Also an inventor, Mr. Sit has been awarded four patents covering a wide range of technical subject matter. He enjoys creative painting and

179

Ikebana, Japanese floral arrangements. Mr. Sit holds a Bachelor of Science degree in mechanical engineering and a Master of Science degree in electrical engineering from the Illinois Institute of Technology, and a Master of Business Administration degree from the Massachusetts Institute of Technology.

Ling Bundgaard is the co-author of *Lateral Approach to Creating Success: Simple Principles for Not Leaving Success to Chance Whether You Manage a Small Shop or a Million Dollar Corporation*, *Lateral Approach to Managing Projects: Simple Principles for Achieving High Customer Satisfaction and Mutual Profitability*, and *Lateral Approach to Taking Charge: Simple Principles for New Bosses on Building Authority and Partnerships*.

During her 31-year tenure at Intel Corporation, Ms. Bundgaard managed many large projects. As General Manager, she started up the first manufacturing plant in Shanghai, China, establishing the first major corporate commitment from Intel inside China. Ms Bundgaard also managed several large cross-cultural projects in other countries including the Philippines and Denmark.

Ms. Bundgaard excels at bringing people and information together to solve problems. She has found that people embrace the basic principles in the Lateral Approach book series once they understand how they stand to benefit from these principles. She believes in lifelong learning and enthusiastically shares in her writing her most memorable nuggets from peers, bosses, and mystics in business.